How to be a Successful Traveller

Also by Andrew Wright

In this series:
How to Communicate Successfully
How to Enjoy Paintings
How to be Entertaining
How to Improve Your Mind

with David Betteridge and Michael Buckby:
Games for Language Learning

How to be a Successful Traveller

Andrew Wright

with drawings by the author

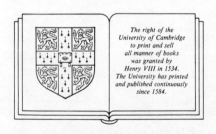

The right of the
University of Cambridge
to print and sell
all manner of books
was granted by
Henry VIII in 1534.
The University has printed
and published continuously
since 1584.

Cambridge University Press
Cambridge
London   New York   New Rochelle
Melbourne   Sydney

Published by the Press Syndicate of the University of Cambridge
The Pitt Building, Trumpington Street, Cambridge CB2 1RP
32 East 57th Street, New York, NY 10022, USA
10 Stamford Road, Oakleigh, Melbourne 3166, Australia

© Cambridge University Press 1986

First published 1986

Printed in Great Britain
at the Bath Press, Avon

ISBN 0 521 27546 6

SE

Contents

Contents

Thanks

I would like to thank Alison Silver, the editor of this series who has made a significant contribution to each book in terms of content and presentation. I would also like to thank Monica Vincent for her valuable advice, Peter Donovan for his support during the long period of writing and Peter Ducker for his concern for the design and typography. I am also grateful to the teachers and students of Nord Anglia for trying out samples of the texts and giving me useful advice for their improvement.

In a book of this kind one is naturally influenced by a large number of writers, lecturers, friends and acquaintances. However, I should like to acknowledge the following writers and their books in particular: J.M. and M.J. Cohen, *Modern Quotations*, Penguin; *The Oxford Dictionary of Quotations*, Oxford University Press; *The International Thesaurus of Quotations*, Penguin; Brian Moynahan, *Fool's Paradise*, Pan; Peter and Magda Hall, *The Penguin International Travel Handbook*, Penguin; John Hatt, *The Tropical Traveller*, Pan; Ingrid Cranfield (ed.), *The Traveller's Handbook*, Heinemann; Charles F. Ehret and Lynne W. Scanlon, *Overcoming Jet Lag*, Berkley Books, New York; Simon Calder, *Hitch Hiker's Manual*, Vacation Work, Oxford; Eddie McGee, *No Need to Die*, Paul Crompton Ltd.

About this book

How to be a Successful Traveller is one in a series of five books. There are seven chapters, each dealing with a different aspect of travelling. There are several different sections in each chapter, and some will probably be more interesting and relevant to you than others. There is no need to read every section. I hope you will find it all interesting and entertaining, and that your reading of English will improve as well as your travelling.

★ Indicates that there is a question you should think about on your own.
★★ Indicates that if you are reading the book with another person you should talk about this particular question with him or her.

You may be reading the book while studying English in a class, with a teacher, or you may be reading it at home in the evenings, or on a train, or anywhere else – it doesn't matter!

What I do hope is that you enjoy reading about travel and travelling – in English!

A few wise words for travellers

★ Do you agree with any of them?

No man should travel until he has learned the language of the country he visits. Otherwise, he voluntarily makes himself a great baby, – so helpless and so ridiculous.
(Emerson, *Journals*, 1833)

The heaviest luggage for a traveller is an empty purse.
(English Proverb)

He that travels much knows much.
(Thomas Fuller, *Gnomologia*, 1732)

They change their climate, not their soul, who rush across the sea.
(Horace, *Epistles*, 20–8 BC)

Travelling. This makes men wiser, but less happy.
(Thomas Jefferson, letter to Peter Carr, Aug. 10, 1787)

A traveller without knowledge is a bird without wings.
(Sa'di, *Gulistan*, 1258)

He who would travel happily must travel light.
(Saint Exupery, *Wind, Sand, and Stars*, 1939)

For my part, I travel not to go anywhere, but to go. I travel for travel's sake. The great affair is to move.
(Robert Louis Stevenson, *Travels with a Donkey*, 1879)

Travelling – now and then

These are the prints of people who lived 3.6 million years ago. The prints have been fossilised into stone and were discovered in Kenya by Mary Leakey, the anthropologist.

People have always travelled. People have searched for food, fled from danger, and always wondered what is round the next corner, what is over the horizon.

Today we sometimes travel for similar reasons. But we also travel for business, as tourists and to visit friends and relatives. And there must be many other reasons!

More people travel than ever before. For example, in 1982 310 million people went abroad for their holidays, and they spent $100 billion. Tourism is the reason why most people travel. And this includes the British! Almost as many British people spend their holidays in Spain as in the South-West of England (a well-known holiday region). Spain, Greece, Morocco and Ireland earn more from tourism than from anything else. Britain earned £4,194 million from tourism in 1984. British airlines earn £200 million per year from tourism. Even one shop can earn a fortune: Harrods in London earns a very large proportion of its income from overseas visitors.

According to a recent survey, the people who travel the most are in this order: the West Germans, the Americans, the French, the British . . .

(John Reader)

If you would like lots of practical advice about travelling, read the rest of this book!

How to prepare for your journey

**Your papers please . . .
and your money**

DON'T LET IT HAPPEN TO YOU!

Passport

Everybody knows that they must have a passport when they go to another country. But many people wait until the last minute before applying for a new passport or for the renewal of their old one. In Britain it can take up to one month to have a new date stamped in a passport! Before you travel write down the number of your passport, the date of issue and the place of issue, and keep this information safe, perhaps in your diary.

Visa

Sometimes you will need special permission to enter a foreign country and you will have to obtain a visa. Usually your travel agent will tell you if you need a visa. However, if you are in any doubt, you should contact the embassy of the country you want to go to, and ask them.

Here is my visa for Sierra Leone.

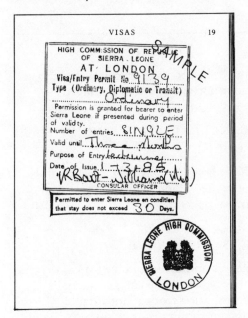

★ How long was I allowed to stay? Here is a visa for the USA.

SOME TIPS

1 If you go to the embassy to get a visa you may have to wait a long time. Make sure you have all the correct papers and information with you, because if you make a mistake you may have to start to queue again! Don't forget you will have to pay for the visa. In some countries you can pay an agent to get you a visa. In Britain Thomas Cook charges £5.00. This is cheap!

2 For many countries in Asia you may have to visit the embassy several times and it may take a week to get a visa. And it may take several weeks to get visas for African countries. Sometimes the embassy sends your application back to their home country. And this, of course, takes a lot of time. So allow a lot of time!

3 You will usually be asked to give a number of passport photographs of yourself. If you are travelling it is a good idea to have a lot of photos with you.

4 There are other possible requirements: you may have to show vaccination certificates; you may have to prove that you are going on holiday and not looking for work.

5 Never stay beyond the date allowed by the visa. You may have to pay a lot of money in fines or you may be put in prison.

Student identity cards

The International Student Identity Card is very useful. Full-time students (of any nationality) may have one and benefit from cheap fares, cheap accommodation, reduced or free entry to museums, etc. To get one, send the following information to your local student travel office:

3

– proof that you are a student, for example, a letter from the college or school which you attend or your student union card. You must also send a passport photograph (signed on the back), with your full name, date of birth and nationality.

Insurance

ILLNESS

Being ill in other countries is expensive. And when you are ill you don't feel you want to think about money. The cost of medical care in the United States is particularly high. An operation and a week or two in hospital might cost $100,000! However, many countries have an agreement to provide free (or cheaper) medical care for foreign visitors from some countries. Ask in your local 'health office' for information; Europeans must use a special form.

LUGGAGE

The airlines don't give you much money if they lose your bags. You might like to pay for insurance in case your luggage is lost or damaged.

CANCELLATION OF YOUR JOURNEY

It is possible to insure against the loss of money if you have to cancel your travel tickets.

CAR INSURANCE

Papers and car insurance for car drivers are essential. You can get the right information from a motoring organisation in your country. You will certainly need your driving licence and often an International Motor Insurance Certificate (Green Card) is necessary. If you are hiring a car make sure you have enough insurance.

★ Which is the best insurance?

A look at the basics

Company	Premium cost	Accident	Cancellation/ curtailment	Illness	Loss or theft of money	Loss or theft of baggage	Comments
AA	£19.60	£100,000	£3,000	£1,000,000	£250	£1,000	Benefits can be doubled for an extra £14.80
Centurion/ American Express	£35.00* £55.00**	£60,000	£50.00	£60,000	***	***	Linked to Europ Assistance
Cornhill	£16.00	£15,000	£3,000	£100,000	£250	£1,000	
Extra Sure	£26.00	£25,000	£1,000	Unlimited	£100	£1,000	Day trip cover for £3.50
General Accident	£16.00	£5,000	£1,500	£100,000	£500	£1,500	Linked to Europ Assistance
Holidaycare	£17.45	£15,000	£1,000	£1,000,000	£300	£1,000	24-hour emergency service
Lloyds Black Horse	£15.60	£5,000	£2,000	£100,000	£200	£1,000	Free insurance extension if necessary
Prutravel	£23.40	£25,000	£5,000	Unlimited	£400	£2,000	Allied to Thomas Cook Travel

  * One year's full cover
 ** One year's full cover for traveller and car
*** Cover varies

Note:
Prices quoted are for 5-8 day cover

■ Sir, Just before departure to the United States my colleague discovered that my travel insurance had a limit of £50,000 to cover sickness and accident. He argued so well that this was not enough that I agreed to increase it with an insurance agent at the airport. Cover for £1,000,000 cost me about £30. I felt that I had made a mistake and we laughed about it most of the way across the Atlantic. Within two days of arriving in the States I had a heart attack which was rather serious. There were complications in which I also caught pneumonia. I was in a very poor condition for several weeks and spent a long time recovering. The bill for this was more than £300,000. If I had not had the insurance cover I could not have paid and would not have been treated. I would, in fact, not be alive today to write this letter. It was for this reason that I felt it was my duty to let other readers of your journal know how important good insurance was for me. I will, fortunately for me, be able to laugh my way over the Atlantic again!

Yours faithfully,
Robin Harley

Medical requirements

Many countries in the world insist that visitors are vaccinated against yellow fever and cholera. The chart on page 7 shows you where there are dangers of these diseases and whether vaccinations are required. However, you must get up to date information from the embassy of the country you are going to, from your travel agent or from your local 'health office'.

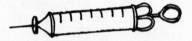

Get advice from your local doctor about two months before you go. (Some vaccinations take several days to become effective.) Make sure you get a vaccination certificate: it must be signed by your doctor and it must be stamped by your local health authority.

Yellow fever This disease is still common in some countries. The vaccination lasts ten years.
Cholera Although cholera is a particularly dangerous disease some countries don't insist on vaccination because the vaccination isn't very effective! Check with the embassy, etc. of the country you are going to.
Malaria This disease is growing more powerful all the time. In 1966 there were 40,000 cases of malaria in India and in 1976 there were 6 million cases! You can get malaria if you are bitten by an infected mosquito. However, you can take tablets each day which will protect you.

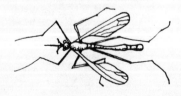

While you are abroad

Have a small first aid kit with you

A packet of adhesive dressings, some insect-repellent and antiseptic creams and water-sterilisation tablets will take up little space and could be useful. But do **not** take any kind of medication to avoid getting diarrhoea unless advised to do so by your doctor.

Make sure drinking water is safe

and the water you use for cleaning your teeth and washing your mouth. Unless you know it is safe – bottled water usually is – sterilise your drinking water. You can do this by boiling the water or by using sterilisation tablets. Milk should be boiled before use unless it is pasteurised or sterilised.

Be careful with these foods

Raw vegetables, salads and unpeeled fruit; raw shellfish; cream, ice cream and ice cubes; under-done meat or fish; and uncooked, cold or reheated food generally can all be contaminated. Freshly cooked foods are safer.

Personal hygiene is vital

Always wash your hands before eating or handling food, particularly if you are camping or caravanning.

The sun can burn your skin faster than you think

The paler your skin, the more quickly and painfully you can be burned, and the more protection you need. For the first day or two allow only 15 minutes direct exposure before covering up. As your tan develops you can allow yourself a little more sun each day, but don't overdo it.

Avoid heat exhaustion

If you rush about and exert yourself too much in a hot climate you will sweat a lot, and your body will lose too much fluid and salt. This can cause headaches, dizziness and nausea. You can prevent this by taking extra salt, drinking plenty of fluid and wearing loose, lightweight clothing – preferably made of cotton or other natural fibres.

VD risks

Sexually transmitted diseases are a serious threat to health throughout the world. If you think you may have been infected, get medical advice and treatment immediately.

Insect pests

Insects spread disease in tropical areas so use insect repellents.

Look at the table of diseases and precautions.

★ Imagine you are going on a business trip for 10 days to Ghana. What vaccinations must you have before you go or what pills must you take with you?

★ Imagine you have won first prize in a competition. You are going to India, China, Indonesia, Japan, New Zealand and Australia. What precautions will you need to take for each country?

★★ If somebody is coming to your country, which, if any, of these illnesses would you warn them about?

Diseases and precautions

	Risk areas	How caught	Vaccination	Vaccination certificate needed?	Revaccination	Other precautions
Cholera	Africa, Asia, Middle East	Contaminated food or water	Usually 2 injections by your doctor	Some countries may require evidence of vaccination within previous 6 months if there have been any cholera outbreaks in countries through which you have travelled. Check before you go	Every 6 months until you return	Vaccination does not guarantee full protection, so take scrupulous care over food and drink
Infectious Hepatitis	Places where sanitation is primitive	Contaminated food or water or contact with an infected person	Get advice from your doctor	No		Take scrupulous care over food, drink and hygiene
Malaria	Africa, Asia, Central and South America	Bite from infected mosquito	None, but anti-malarial tablets are available			
Polio	Everywhere except Australia, New Zealand, Europe, North America	Direct contact with an infected person; rarely by contaminated water or food	3 doses of drops from your doctor, taken at 4-8 week intervals	No	May be needed after 10 years. Ask your doctor	Take scrupulous care over food and drink
Rabies	Many parts of the world	Bite or scratch from infected animal				
Smallpox	None		Not necessary	No (**Smallpox has been eradicated worldwide**)		
Tetanus	Places where medical facilities not readily available	Open injury	Get advice from your doctor	No		Wash any wound thoroughly
Typhoid	Everywhere except Australia, New Zealand, Northern Europe, North America	Contaminated food, water or milk	2 injections from your doctor, at an interval of 4-6 weeks. If you have to go abroad urgently, the interval can be reduced to 10 days	No	Usually after 3 years (one injection only)	Take scrupulous care over food and drink
Yellow Fever	Africa, South America	Bite from infected mosquito	1 injection at a Yellow Fever Vaccination Centre, at least 10 days before you go abroad. To make an appointment telephone your nearest centre	Some countries may ask for a certificate if you have passed through a country where yellow fever is present. Check before you go	After 10 years	Avoid mosquito bites, as for malaria

Are traveller's cheques a good idea?

Many travellers carry traveller's cheques instead of cash. In some countries you can actually use the cheques instead of cash . . . you don't need to go to a bank to change the cheques into money but the shopkeeper, etc. will accept them as money.

You buy traveller's cheques from a bank in your own country, and then exchange them for cash in any bank in the country you are visiting. When you take your cheques to a bank the clerk will ask to see your passport and will compare your signature on the cheque with the one on the passport. Probably the most useful cheques are in American dollars. Sterling cheques are accepted in most countries; they are sometimes not accepted in the United States.

If you lose your cheques or if they are stolen the bank will give you your money back. Some banks or agencies give you the money very quickly if the cheques are stolen and some take a very long time. So, before you buy the cheques, ask the bank how they will pay you if the cheques are lost. Some banks don't pay you until you return home! Thomas Cook and American Express have agencies in every country and they are ready to pay you quickly when you need help. American Express try to pay within 24 hours.

What about credit cards?

These cards are very useful . . . although they do tempt you to spend a lot of your money because they are so easy to use! Wherever you are, good hotels will let you stay, car hire firms will let you hire their cars, and airlines will let you buy their tickets with a credit card.

For just £10 a year – any member of your family can also enjoy all these benefits.

- The Card welcomed by over 700,000 establishments – hotels, restaurants, ticket offices, shops, garages and service stations – throughout the world... with over 60,000 of them in the United Kingdom and Ireland alone.

- Freedom from dependence on cash or frequent cheque transactions.

- Freedom from bother with currency exchanges when travelling.

- Up to £35,000 Travel Accident Insurance at no extra cost when travel tickets are charged to the Card. (*Insurance offered through American Express and subject to conditions of cover.)

- Car hire usually without deposit... theatre bookings by telephone.

- Privilege assistance from the world's largest travel service, including cheque-cashing facilities at many branches worldwide.

- Special Cardmember benefits, exclusive to American Express, such as Medex Assistance when travelling overseas. (Full details on request.)

- *Please allow up to 28 days after receipt of Card for delivery of wallet.*

American Express Europe Ltd. P.O. Box 76, Brighton, Sussex BN2 1YW.

Should I take some cash?

It is always useful to have some cash, particularly if it is a world currency. American dollars are the best, as they are readily accepted all around the world.

Try to take some cash of the country you are going to. When you arrive in a foreign country the banks may be closed and you may have to pay a taxi driver or make a phone call. However, it is usually easy to change money at the airport when you arrive.

Don't forget   Write down the numbers and the relevant names and addresses of all your papers . . . your passport, traveller's cheques, camera number, etc., etc. Keep one set of numbers with you and leave one at home with a friend.

9

How to decide what to take

Your clothes

Which clothes for which month?

★ Look at the following maps and charts.

1 Which place has temperature and rainfall most like the region where you live?

2 Which place is completely different?!

3 Which is the driest, which the wettest, and which the coldest and the hottest?

4 Which place would you like to go to? When would you like to go? And what sort of clothes would you take?

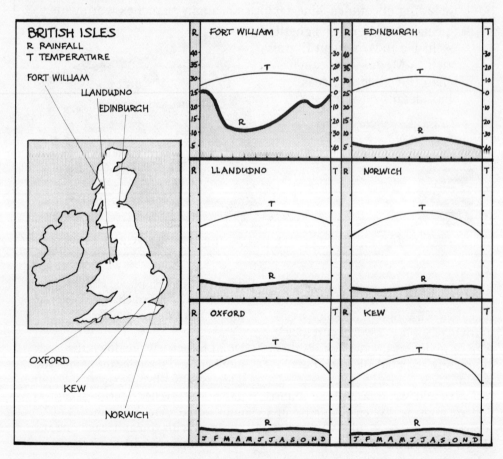

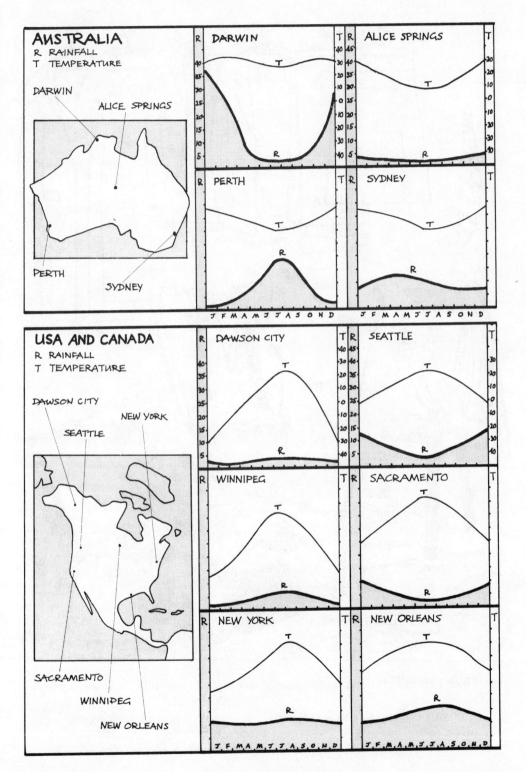

AUSTRALIA
R RAINFALL
T TEMPERATURE

DARWIN

ALICE SPRINGS

PERTH

SYDNEY

DARWIN

ALICE SPRINGS

PERTH

SYDNEY

J F M A M J J A S O N D

USA AND CANADA
R RAINFALL
T TEMPERATURE

DAWSON CITY

NEW YORK

SEATTLE

DAWSON CITY

SEATTLE

WINNIPEG

SACRAMENTO

NEW YORK

NEW ORLEANS

SACRAMENTO

WINNIPEG

NEW ORLEANS

J F M A M J J A S O N D

J F M A M J J A S O N D

Checklists

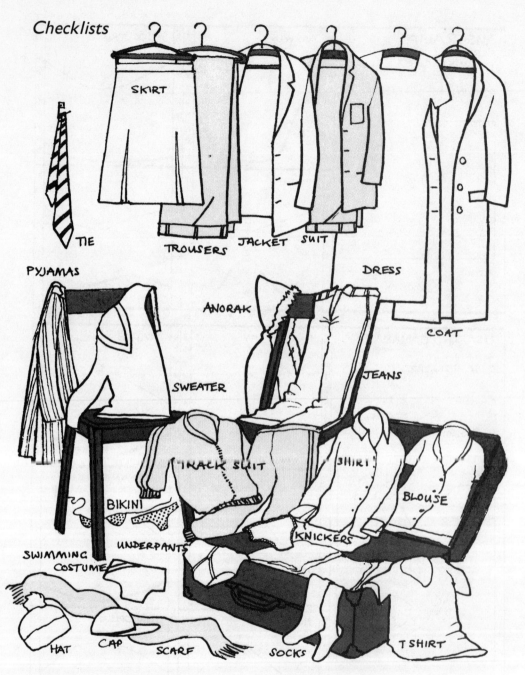

SKIRT · TIE · TROUSERS · JACKET · SUIT · DRESS · COAT · PYJAMAS · ANORAK · SWEATER · JEANS · TRACK SUIT · SHIRT · BLOUSE · BIKINI · KNICKERS · UNDERPANTS · SWIMMING COSTUME · HAT · CAP · SCARF · SOCKS · T SHIRT

★ Which items of clothing would you take:
– on a two week trip to Britain staying in hotels?
– on a three week trip to Scotland . . . on a walking holiday and staying in Youth Hostels?
– on a six week hitchhiking trip (see page 30) through Europe?
Is there anything missing?

MIRROR
SOAP
TOOTHPASTE
TOOTHBRUSH
WET RAZOR
RAZOR
SHAVING SOAP
DEODORANT
MAKE UP
PERFUME
LIPSTICK
SHAMPOO
BRUSH
HAIR ROLLERS
HAIR SPRAY
SAFETY PIN
HAIR DRYER
FACECLOTH
HAND TOWEL
TORCH
BOTTLE OPENER
KNIFE
SCISSORS
CORKSCREW
COMPASS
PRESENT
VACUUM FLASK
ELASTIC BAND
NEEDLE
COTTON
SUNGLASSES
STRING
LAVATORY PAPER
KNIFE FORK SPOON
EAR PLUGS
EYE SHADES
SHOE POLISH

★ Which kinds of clothing would you recommend visitors to bring to your country (men, women and children and in any season)? Decide just what sort of people they are and what they are going to do.

★★ Choose a person you know and pack (write a list of things) for him or her as if they were going to Britain, the USA, Canada or Australia. Check the climate charts on pages 10 and 11. Compare lists with your partner and explain the reasons for the differences.

WHAT DOES SHE TAKE?

Alison Gee

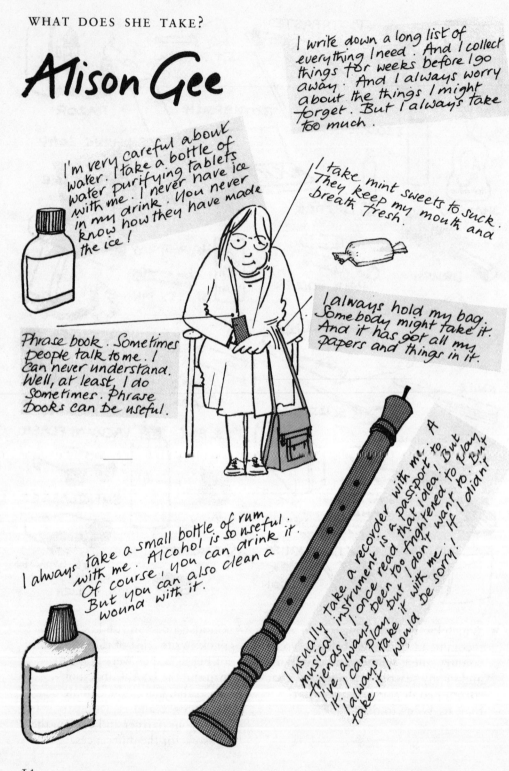

I write down a long list of everything I need. And I collect things for weeks before I go away. And I always worry about the things I might forget. But I always take too much.

I'm very careful about water. I take a bottle of water purifying tablets with me. I never have ice in my drink. You never know how they have made the ice!

I take mint sweets to suck. They keep my mouth and breath fresh.

I always hold my bag. Somebody might take it. And it has got all my papers and things in it.

Phrase book. Sometimes people talk to me. I can never understand. Well, at least I do sometimes. Phrase books can be useful.

I always take a small bottle of rum with me. Alcohol is so useful. Of course, you can drink it. But you can also clean a wound with it.

I usually take a recorder with me. A musical instrument is a passport to friends! I once read that idea. But I've always been too frightened to play. But I can play. But I don't want to. But I always take it with me. If I didn't take it I would be sorry!

Your luggage

What should you choose?

SUITCASE

The advantage of a suitcase is that you can lay your clothes flat. The disadvantage of a suitcase is that it is difficult to carry!

A good suitcase is expensive. On the other hand a good suitcase will last a long time and many journeys. Airline porters often throw suitcases on top of each other and many cases are damaged. My own suitcase is made of a very strong fibre and it has lasted for ten years.

You are usually allowed to take one or two cases on a plane. (Different airlines have different rules: sometimes the rule is one or two cases; sometimes the rule is that the total length, breadth and depth must not be more than 260mm; and sometimes the rule is based on the weight, e.g. maximum 21 kilos.)

SHOULDER CASE

The advantage of a shoulder case is that you can carry it easily, and at the same time you can keep your clothes flat.

CARRY ON BAG

A carry on bag (called a carry on bag because you are allowed to carry it on to the aeroplane) is essential for all air travellers. (And I believe it is very useful for all travellers for similar reasons.) A carry on bag must not be larger than: 450 mm × 350 mm × 150 mm, and you must be able to fit it under your seat on the plane. You can buy carry on bags specially made for travellers; they have a variety of pockets for your papers, your money, your address book, etc.

WHEELS

small wheels get stuck in holes

I can make the handle much shorter.

You can buy little wheels to fit onto the bottom of your case. These wheels are very helpful. However, they are only successful on smooth floors. I believe it is better to have bigger wheels. You can then pull your case along rough pavements in town.

FRAMED BACKPACK OR RUCKSACK

A framed backpack or rucksack is ideal for people who walk and camp. However, it is not ideal for other travellers! If you have ever tried to stand on a crowded tube train next to someone carrying a giant framed backpack you will know what I mean! The various straps and objects fastened on the outside all poke you in the face. And if you want to hitchhike then your backpack may be on your knees and you won't be able to see anything. If you are going to travel on public transport or hitchhike it is better to have a backpack with the frame inside the pack.

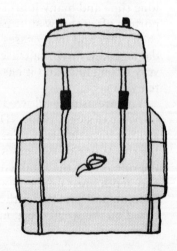

HOLDALL

Alternatively, travellers by train, bus or hitchhiking might prefer to carry a holdall. Modern holdalls are very light and they can hold a lot of things. You can easily push a holdall into a small space under a seat or on a luggage rack. Furthermore, you can put your arms through the straps and wear the bag like a backpack.

How to protect your luggage against thieves

There are thieves everywhere! Airports are famous for thefts from travellers' luggage. It is obviously a good idea if you lock your case. However, never leave any valuable things in it like your money, passport, camera, etc. Thieves know how to open locks – it is their job!

Lock the ends of the zip fasteners on your bags. Backpackers sometimes take a chain and lock with them. They can then lock their bag to a railing or chair, etc. (although it would be easy to cut the strap with a knife!).

How to label your luggage

Write your name and address on each piece of luggage. It is better to write on the luggage than on a label as labels can be torn off. Sometimes thieves tear off the label and sell it to other thieves who then go to your home while you are away.

If your luggage looks like other peoples' luggage then it is a good idea to make it different; you can put a coloured shape on the side of it. People often take luggage which doesn't belong to them; they think it is theirs.

★★ What sort of luggage have you got? Is it satisfactory or would you like something else?

How to enjoy travelling by air and by thumb

Fares: cheap, cheaper, cheapest

You are on a plane and you are flying from London to Los Angeles. You have paid £1,256 for your return journey. It is a full fare economy ticket. There are 307 other passengers on the plane with you. Have all the others who are sitting with you paid the same price (£628 single) for their tickets? Certainly not!

You have paid more than many of the people around you! Even some passengers who are sitting in the first class compartment have paid less money than you!

1 Guido de Valdonna is a famous conductor. His orchestra is going to play for one week in Los Angeles. The city of Los Angeles is paying for his flight and, of course, they want to give him a pleasant journey and they want

to show their respect for him. So they have bought a first class return ticket and they have not tried to get a cheaper price. At least his ticket cost more than yours even though he didn't have to pay for it. The ticket cost £2,910.

2 Mrs Mary Whitethorn is a widow. She has just lost her husband and now she wants to get away from home and her unhappy loss. She has decided to go on a world tour. She has bought a first class Round the World ticket which cost £2,499. This part of Mrs Whitethorn's journey i.e. from London to Los Angeles, is costing £558. (The price of this fare is dependent on her completing all the stages in her journey.)

3 Mr Harvey B. Hoover is rich and has retired from business. He is used to travelling and he has many friends in different countries. If he hasn't got a friend in the place where he has arrived then he can easily pay for a hotel. He too is doing a world tour. He has bought a first class ticket but he is a 'standby' passenger: this means that he can't be sure of getting on the plane. (Mrs Whitethorn would be very anxious if she didn't know for sure whether she could get on the plane!) The standby first class ticket costs much less than Mrs Whitethorn's ticket and this part of the journey costs £444. (This price also depends on him completing his journey round the world.)

4 Brian Jones is a book publisher. In a few weeks he is going to Rome. However, he knew he wanted to go to Los Angeles first so he bought a ticket London – Los Angeles – London – Rome – London. Now he is using the first part of his ticket (London – Los Angeles – London), which is costing him £818. Mr Jones has paid the price of a return ticket from London to Los Angeles and added on Rome at a cheaper rate than the full price.

5 This information is going to be very painful for you! It is bad enough for you to learn that Brian Jones is paying £438 less than you. Peter Wood is paying nothing at all! Peter Wood is a journalist. A travel magazine has asked him to do a series of articles on holidays in the United States. Peter Wood has asked the public relations department in the airline to give him a complementary ticket and the department has agreed.

6 Elizabeth Meyer has an APEX ticket. It cost £516. APEX means Advanced Purchase Excursion Fare. Ms Meyer had to plan her journey 21 days ago and she had to pay the full cost of her ticket straightaway. Also she can only travel on this plane, the one you are on; if she had missed the plane she couldn't get on another unless she paid more for it. If, for example, she had driven to the airport and her car had broken down and she had arrived too late for the plane then the airline would have had no sympathy for her! However, she is on the plane and she is paying much less than you.

7 Monica Reeves has paid £210. She bought the ticket from a travel agent who had a contract with the airline. The agent had to buy ten tickets for each of several flights and then try to sell them. These are called Scheduled Consolidated Fares and agents always offer a good price for the tickets.

It isn't pleasant to sit next to someone who may have paid much less than you. How can you find the cheapest fare? First of all do you want the cheapest fare? Do you mind taking a risk? For most people the best advice is to go to a travel agent.

If a travel agent thinks that you are asking a lot of people for advice then he or she will probably try to find a good price for you. In Britain the best travel agents are often to be found in universities. They know how to find the cheapest fares (and anyone can go to a Student Travel Service to buy a ticket).

Some travel magazines are very helpful, for example, *Business Traveller* often contains useful advice about cheap tickets.

How to read your ticket

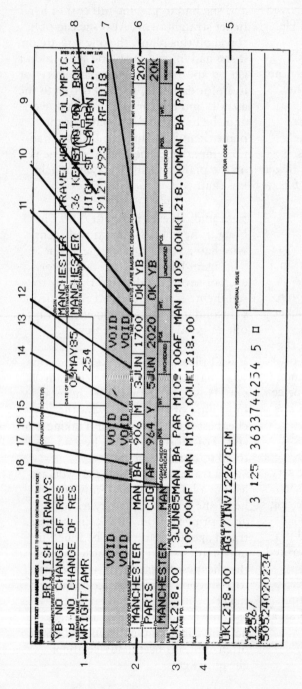

Most tickets are very similar to the one shown. And most tickets are written in English: English is the language of air travel. What do all the different parts mean? Is the ticket correct? How do you find out if the flight, date and time are correct? What other information can you find out from your ticket?

1 *Name:* This must be your name! You can't give or sell your ticket to anyone else! (Note: AMR means Mr A!)

2 *Good for Passage:* Each page in the ticket is different. Make sure they are correct. The heavy black lined box on each page tells you where you are going from and to.

3 *Fare:* This is what you have paid for your ticket.

4 *Tax:* There may be an airport tax.

5 *Tour Code:* If you are on a package holiday the reference number is written here.

6 *Allow:* Usually you can take between 20 and 30 kilos without extra cost. In the United States the number of cases is the important factor and not their weight.

7 *Fare Basis:* This is the type of fare. In this case YB means 'Euro Budget'.

8 *Flight Coupon:* This is the 'page' number of your 'ticket book'. This is Flight Coupon 3.

9 *Ticket Number*

10 *Status:* It should be marked OK. If it isn't then ask why not.

11 *Time:* This is the local time. Usually airlines use a 24 hour clock. In the United States they use a 12 hour clock and add 'A' for morning and 'P' for after midday.

12 *Date:* This is your departure date. Make sure it is correct!

13 *Date of Issue:* The date when you paid for the ticket.

14 *Class:* M and Y mean 'economy class', C means 'club class', F means 'first class'. If you have paid for first class or club class and there is an M on your ticket then complain!

15 *Flight:* This is your flight number and it is important to you. (Don't ask for the 1700 flight to Paris but for flight BA 906.)

16 *Conjunction Ticket:* If you are going on a long journey you may stop in four or more different places. You will need another ticket book: this is the reference.

17 *Carrier:* Each airline is represented by two or three letters. For example, BA for British Airways, AF for Air France. So my ticket shows that I went from Manchester to Paris by British Airways and from Paris to Manchester by Air France.

18 *Baggage Checked/Unchecked:* The number of cases, etc. and their weight must be written down. If the information is not written down and your cases are lost you will not get compensation.

★★ Tell your partner everything you can find out about this journey from the ticket shown here: about the journey, the fares and the restrictions.

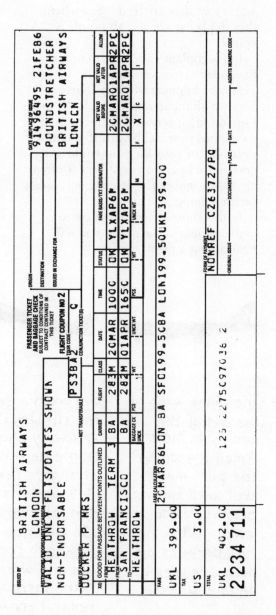

How to translate aeroplane noises

Are you frightened of flying? Many people are! One in every three people admit that they are frightened when they fly! What are you afraid of? A crash?

But aeroplanes are safer than cars. Every day 2,500 aeroplanes fly 1,040,000 kilometres in the United States without an accident. Lloyds in London say it is twenty times more dangerous to travel by car. If you flew every day of your life you would only crash once in 1,000 years! Fear is often caused by ignorance. Strange noises can be frightening.

In this short section I will try to explain some of the noises you will hear during a flight.

4 The plane isn't climbing so steeply. The engines are suddenly quiet! Have they stopped? Will you drop like a stone?

1 The plane waits at the end of the runway. Is there something wrong? The pilot must wait until he has permission to leave. When he has permission he increases the engine speed.

2 Before the end of the runway the plane suddenly changes angle and the noise changes. The Boeing 747, for example, can take off at 290 km per hour. Although the engines are still working very hard there is less noise because the wheels aren't on the ground.

3 The plane is rising steeply. The houses and roads are already quite small. Then there are two bangs! Have you hit a cloud!? The pilot folds the wheels into the plane. The plane can go faster without wheels and save a lot of fuel.

5 The plane is rising and falling, the glass of orange juice is spilling onto the table in front of you. There is turbulence in the air. The pilot must take the plane higher. And, of course, the engines work harder again.

6 A long way from the airport, perhaps 300 kilometres, the plane begins to descend. The noise of the engines may sound quieter.

7 A very shallow angle of descent saves a lot of fuel. A steep angle of descent may cost 360-450 litres more petrol. In order to slow down the pilot changes the shape of the wings. He also lowers the wheels.

8 Nearly on the runway! The front of the plane rises and a moment later the wheels hit the runway. Suddenly the engines make a loud noise! As the wheels touch the runway the pilot lifts the spoilers in the wings. And he puts the engines into reverse.

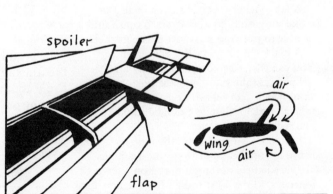

spoiler

flap

air

wing

air

★★ Do you enjoy flying? Have you ever felt nervous during a flight?
★★ Can you think of other occasions when a strange noise might frighten you?

How to be comfortable

Yvonne Guy is a make-up artist. She travels to many countries, as she does the make-up of film actors and actresses and advertising models. She gave me a lot of useful advice for travellers. How much of this advice is relevant to you?

'First of all I always wear loose, comfortable shoes when I am travelling by air because my feet swell up: I think everyone's do. I try to sit with my feet up as much as possible. I always take warm socks on the plane. The floors are often very cold. The heating changes, it goes up and down.

The most comfortable clothing is a tracksuit. It is soft and loose, and you can open or close it very easily . . . it has a zip. You should wear a T shirt under a jersey or tracksuit top. Then, if you are hot you can take the jersey off and still look OK.

I always take a big scarf with me. Then I can wrap it around me if I feel cold. When you get tired you get cold.

A long jacket is better than a coat. But make sure it has good pockets. You should be able to put your passport in the pockets.

A black sleeping mask is very useful. You can then sleep even if it is daylight.

I always take some moisturiser for my skin, which gets very dry on a plane. And take a bottle of Eau de Cologne to make you feel fresh and clean.

I often take a walkman; the tape recorder fits in my pocket and the earphones really are very light. I never get bored on journeys. I love West Indian Reggae music.

I often manicure my nails as well. It kills an hour! Oh yes, and I write a lot of letters on the plane.

The meals are always disgusting on the plane . . . they are always so stodgy . . . and tasteless. Personally, I only eat fruit, oranges, bananas . . . and I drink fruit juice as well.'

How to exercise on a plane

★ Try these exercises now!
Sit as straight as you can, pull in your stomach, open out your chest, make your neck as vertical as possible, lift your head high but keep your chin in. Breathe in deeply, hold your breath for five seconds then slowly relax and breathe out. Repeat this action five times. Then make the muscles in your legs hard. Hold for five seconds. Relax. Repeat.

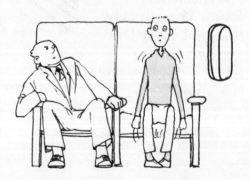

Walk up and down the aisle.

If you aren't self-conscious, do the following exercises at the back of the plane or in the extra space by the emergency door.

If you are self-conscious, you can do small stretching exercises in the toilet. Careful! I once pushed against the door and fell out.
Note that as you sit for a long time your spine bends and traps the discs.

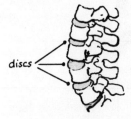

So it is important to bend the other way at least once an hour to let the disc return to its place. This is particularly important for some back complaints.

Turn your shoulders in circles, five times to the front and five times to the back.

Turn your head five times to the right and five to the left.

Turn your feet five times clockwise and five times anti-clockwise.

Do the same with your hands.

How to avoid jet lag

(If you fly over several time zones you may not feel well! This is called 'jet lag'.)

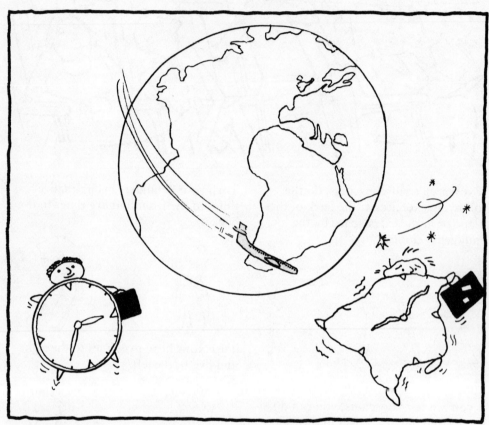

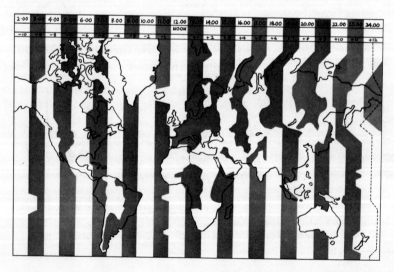

★ Imagine you are in London. You want to phone your family during *their* evening. What time should you phone by British time?

What is jet lag?

YOUR BODY CLOCK

Your body works like a clock, like a 24 hour clock. Most people follow a regular pattern of activities every day. They wake up, get up, wash, dress, have breakfast, leave home, etc., at the same time every day. And the day is fixed by the clock and by the light.

The time of the day and the light aren't changed if we fly north or south. For these reasons we can fly thousands of miles north or south and not suffer from jet lag. But if we fly eastwards or westwards 15% of travellers are severely upset and the rest of us are affected to some extent.

Dr K.E. Klein and his associates at the Institute for Flight Medicine in Bad Godesberg, Germany, have measured people's mental performance at different times of the day. They have found that it is highest between two and four in the afternoon. Reaction times and physical movement are at their best then. The worst time is between two and four in the morning. Researchers in industry say that night workers make more mistakes than day workers and have more illnesses due to mental tension.

When we suddenly arrive in a new time zone we are expected to eat, sleep and work at times when our body wishes to do different things. Of course, we get used to the new day, but it takes time! After crossing six or seven time zones we may not sleep normally for four or five days. Our heartbeat (which is usually faster in the day than at night) may take five or six days to become normal, our ability to think may take from two days to two weeks to settle down!

I flew to Honolulu from Britain recently. Honolulu is 11 hours behind British summer time. At 7 o'clock in the morning in Honolulu I had my breakfast . . . but my mind and body were expecting my afternoon tea!

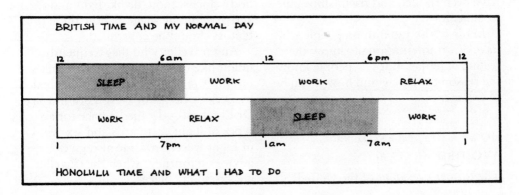

Jet set success may give you jet lag!

Paul Hill is 28. He is already a senior representative of a major film and television lighting company. He travels for his company throughout the world. He is successful and he is very fit! He runs at least 8 kilometres every day. He swims, plays tennis and in the winter he plays football. Furthermore, he enjoys parachuting whenever he has the opportunity! But jet lag can make him feel very tired and strange.

'When I travel by plane and cross three or four time zones, I can't think clearly, I forget things, I can't respond quickly in traffic and sometimes I can't even see very well!'

Jet lag mistakes

The former United States Secretary of State, John Foster Dulles, said that he had made a number of unwise decisions due to jet lag. One wonders how many other decisions which have affected the future of nations and millions of people have been unwisely made. How many athletes and musicians have failed to do their best? How many business people have been slow and unable to think with speed and imagination? How many holidays have been spoiled and friendships put in difficulties?

Many of the 140 million people who have flown internationally know the feeling of jet lag. But few people know the reason for jet lag and how it can be overcome.

HOW A US PRESIDENT
AVOIDED JET LAG

The former president of the United States, Mr Lyndon Johnson had one answer. He took his day with him! For example, when he flew to South Vietnam to discuss matters with President Thieu he insisted on eating, sleeping and working his own American day. It was very inconvenient for everyone else but it provided one answer.

Some pilots and air crew try to use the same system. They keep their watches at home time and try to live home hours of work and sleep.

The three step jet lag programme

The Three Step Jet Lag Programme has been developed by Dr Charles F. Ehret of Argonne's Division of Biological and Medical Research. It is the most thorough and helpful technique available. The basic idea of the programme is summarised below. However, many details of information for each journey must be considered, for example:

1 Whether you are flying eastwards or westwards . . . because eastwards brings you more problems.
2 The time you leave.
3 The time you arrive.
4 The number of time zones you cross. Ehret says that four things affect our body clocks: food, drink, light and activity; and he suggests how these four factors should be controlled.

Any traveller who flies frequently might like to buy a copy of Dr Ehret's book, *Overcoming Jet Lag*, published by Berkley Books of New York in 1983. Dr Ehret gives detailed advice for six types of flight eastwards and six types of flight westwards. He also gives advice on journeys when the traveller goes to many places.

The three step jet lag programme

BEFORE THE FLIGHT

For several days before the flight you should control what you eat and drink. Basically, you should alternate one day with a lot of protein and one day with very little.

DAY ONE

You should eat food which is rich in protein, for example, meat, eggs, beans; in the evening eat carbohydrates, for example, spaghetti, pancakes, potatoes, etc. You should only drink coffee between 3 and 5 pm.

DAY TWO

You shouldn't eat very much! And the food should be light, for example, fruit, light soup, salad, toast without butter. You should only drink coffee between 3 and 5 pm.

EXAMPLES

If your flight crosses three or four time zones, Ehret suggests you start only the day before the flight with a day of high protein food. However, for a flight crossing seven or eight time zones you should start three days before the flight with a day of high protein food, followed by a day with little protein and then another rich in protein.

DURING THE FLIGHT

You must get used to the time of the country you are going to. Create the day and night of the country you are going to on the plane: set your watch to the 'new' time. Wear an eye shade during the 'new' night and put on the light during the 'new' day. During the 'new' day which you create on the plane you should be active; you should read, talk to your neighbour, walk up and down the aisle and do exercises!

Food: you should try to eat according to the times of your 'new' day. The midday meal during your 'new' day should be high in protein and the evening meal of your 'new' day should be high in carbohydrates. Drink plenty of water or fruit juice on the flight.

AFTER THE FLIGHT

You must copy the daily pattern of the local people. Have plenty of coffee in the morning but no more during the day. Don't sleep during the day and go to bed at 10 o'clock and try to sleep.

Hitchhiking

Hitchhiking is the cheapest but probably least reliable method of travelling. You can never predict when you are going to reach your destination. You may have to wait a very long time for someone to stop and pick you up, and you never know how far they can take you. However, you meet a great variety of people, and travel in all sorts of vehicles, from enormous lorries to expensive cars.

An interview with an experienced hitchhiker

Andrew Wright: Do you hitchhike to save money or do you hitchhike for some other reason?

Duncan Bennett: I haven't got any money to save! I'm a student. If I didn't hitchhike I wouldn't be able to travel. And I think it's very important to travel. It's particularly important for a young person. So really, the answer to your question is that I hitchhike in order to travel and, of course, to meet people.

AW: So you don't feel you're a beggar?

DB: No, certainly not. When I stand by the road I'm saying, I would like to travel with you, would you like to travel with me?

AW: Is it easy to get a lift? Do people stop or do you have to wait a very long time?

DB: It depends where you are, what time it is and how many people are with you and whether they are men or women!

AW: Is it best by yourself or with others?

DB: I'll do you a sketch . . .

AW: Isn't it dangerous for a woman to hitchhike by herself?

DB: Yes. On the other hand a lot of things are dangerous. It is very dangerous to travel in a car. And, in any case, most people in Britain will be respectful of her right to travel as she wants. But I agree it is a bit more dangerous and I prefer my girlfriend to hitch with me or with one of our friends.

AW: And is it faster for you if you travel with a woman?

DB: Yes, it's certainly faster.

AW: Can you give any advice to people from other countries?

DB: Yes, first of all, try it! Britain is one of the best countries for hitching. Only Germany is better.

Duncan then gave a list of Dos and Don'ts.

DO

– Plan your route.
– Make sure that when you are travelling on a motorway you get out of the car at a service station or off the motorway altogether.
– Make sure you stand in a place where drivers can see you clearly and where it is safe for them to stop.

AVERAGE WAITING TIME

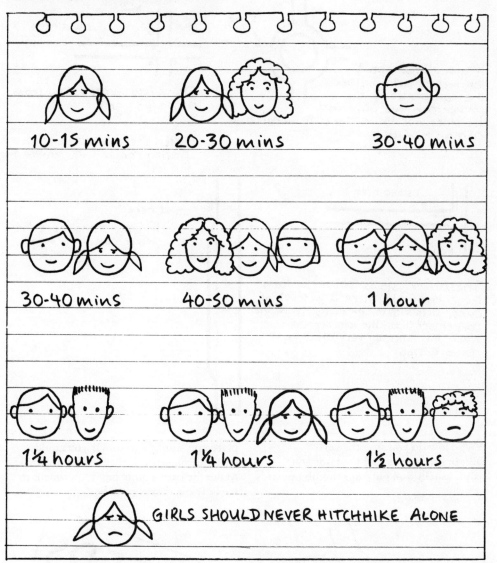

10-15 mins   20-30 mins   30-40 mins

30-40 mins   40-50 mins   1 hour

1¼ hours   1¼ hours   1½ hours

GIRLS SHOULD NEVER HITCHHIKE ALONE

DON'T

– Stand beyond a motorway sign which looks like this.

(You aren't actually allowed to hitch on motorways, though you can use them as they are the fastest way of travelling. The best place to stand is in a service station.)
– Stand on a long, straight stretch of road. The cars are going very fast and it is difficult for the drivers to stop.

THE BEST WAY

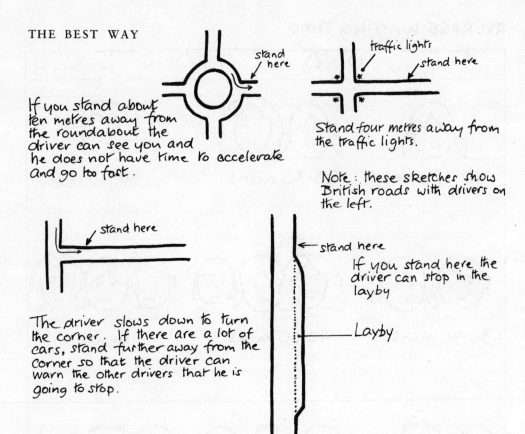

If you stand about ten metres away from the roundabout the driver can see you and he does not have time to accelerate and go too fast.

stand here

traffic lights
stand here

Stand four metres away from the traffic lights.

Note: these sketches show British roads with drivers on the left.

stand here

The driver slows down to turn the corner. If there are a lot of cars, stand further away from the corner so that the driver can warn the other drivers that he is going to stop.

stand here

If you stand here the driver can stop in the layby

Layby

AW: How do you stop the cars?
DB: In Britain you just hold out your hand, usually you put your thumb upwards like this . . .

place you want to go to. Or you could write the name of the nearest big town. Make the letters quite big. Experiment to see how big they should be.

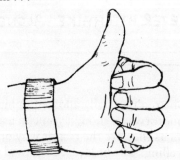

Actually, the best system is to have a sign. You have a piece of white card or better still you have a piece of thin wood or plastic. Then you write on the card the

LEEDS PLEASE

Note the polite 'please'!

AW: What about clothes?

DB: You can make yourself look very different if you want to. I know someone who always hitched wearing a suit and carrying an umbrella. He did very well. Occasionally, people dress up as monkeys or things like that . . .

AW: You said there are good and bad times for hitchhiking?

DB: The best time is during the week . . .

and during the daytime. You get most lifts from working people: lorry drivers, commercial travellers, etc. If you are going on a long journey then start very early, even as early as 5 o'clock in the morning. At that time the lorry drivers are setting off on their long journeys and may be looking for someone to talk to. Families don't usually pick you up.

AW: Any more tips?

DB: Well, you learn all kinds of things when you do it. The main advice is, try it! You'll meet a lot of different people. And you'll learn a lot about the country.

★★ Have you ever hitchhiked? Is it allowed in your country and is it a recognised way of travelling? Would you give any extra or different advice to a person hitching in your country?

★★ Have you ever given a hitchhiker a lift? Do you like the idea of hitching?

Boats, rail, coaches and cars

Air travel and hitchhiking are the two extremes of travel. Travel by boat, rail, coach and car are probably known to most people. For visitors coming to Britain from other European countries there are boats which arrive at Newcastle, Hull, Harwich, Dover, Southampton, Portsmouth, Plymouth and others. Some of these boats are 'car ferries'.

Travel by train in Britain is expensive. A single ticket from London to Manchester which is about 320 km costs £22.50. There are cheap tickets on some trains and it is a good idea to ask about these. Note that it is possible to

take bicycles on most trains in Britain without any extra cost. Good news for cyclists!

Coaches connect the major cities, and local bus services are also quite good. Long distance coach services are cheaper than trains; London to Manchester costs about £11.00.

Cars? In Britain traffic still drives on the left. If you haven't tried to drive on the 'wrong' side of the road then you might think it would be very difficult. In fact, people get used to it very quickly. After all, British people cross over to France and Belgium in their cars and they have to learn to drive on the right. The greatest danger is when motorists stop at a café, etc. and then start off again and forget to drive on the right side, i.e. the left side!

How to look after yourself and other people

Going out with people

What sort of places do people go to for a drink and a chat?
In Britain, of course, it is very common to go to a pub at lunch time or in the evening.
In Australia: bars, restaurants, cafés, night clubs.
In Canada: as in Australia, and including coffee shops.
In the United States: as above but including coffee bars and coffee clubs. There is no need for formal membership of a coffee club.
Can women go to such places by themselves?

In each country the answer is, Yes, but it isn't very common.
At what time do people usually go for dinner in a restaurant?
In Australia people go for dinner as early as 6.30. In Britain, Canada and the United States it is more usual to have dinner at about 8.00.
What sort of clothes do people usually wear when they go out for the evening?
Australians are relaxed people and usually dress informally when going out for dinner. However, a jacket and tie are essential for men and a dress for women in more expensive restaurants.
In Canada a suit for men is still normal. In the United States men would wear a

---

Do you give tips?

AUSTRALIA

Tipping is not general in Australia. Restaurants might include a service charge.

BRITAIN

10% is the guide for taxi drivers, 10% to 15% for a waiter depending on the cost of the meal.

CANADA

10% to 15% in restaurants and bars; 50 cents to cloakroom

attendants and railway porters; taxi drivers expect 12% to 15% and hotel staff 75 cents to one dollar.

UNITED STATES

Tipping is important: taxi drivers 15% (never less than 50 cents); a waiter 15% (or 10% if he or she wasn't very good!); hotel porters 50 cents per bag and 50 cents for opening your bedroom door, etc.; the doorman 50 cents for each bag and 25 cents if he calls a taxi for you; the chambermaid (room cleaner) 5 dollars for a stay of a week.

---

jacket and tie, although a tie is increasingly less important.

In Britain habits are changing rapidly. However, if you are invited to a smart restaurant you should wear formal clothes, at least a jacket and tie if you are a man. On the other hand, it is very common to see men wearing an open-necked shirt or a jersey in restaurants and at other people's houses.

Are there any social customs which people should know about?

Australia and Canada are completely independent countries in spite of their close connections with Britain. It would be quite mistaken and most annoying if this were not recognised by a visitor.

Australia is famous for sport; however, the arts are also very strong and individual. Be careful how you refer to Australian life!

★ What would you tell a visitor about tipping and customs in your country?

How to survive problems

Thieves

There are more and more thieves in every country. Small thefts are annoying and perhaps emotionally disturbing. Bigger thefts can ruin your journey or your holiday.

PICKPOCKETS

These are thieves who steal from people's pockets. Pickpockets usually work in a gang of two or three. Very often two of the gang bump into you. You look at them, and probably protest. Meanwhile, the other pickpocket takes your money or your papers. Pickpockets sometimes do their thieving in theatres and restaurants too.

SNATCHERS

Snatchers take something from you very quickly and run away. They may take your purse, your handbag, your shoulder bag or your camera.

Sometimes snatchers are motorcyclists.

Some advice: Shoulder bags aren't safe for your valuables, your money, passport, etc. Snatchers take them, pickpockets get into them or cut them open. Back trouser pockets are the least safe! Front trouser pockets are probably the best. Money belts are good although they can make you fat, and it is difficult to get your money without getting half undressed. Nevertheless they are one of the safest methods!

MUGGING

Sometimes a thief or several thieves take hold of you. Perhaps they hit you and ask you for your money. This crime is increasing. In London, for example there were 8,700 muggings and robberies in 1974 and 22,100 muggings and robberies in 1983. In New York mugging is very common!

The advice is: Remain calm, perhaps friendly, give the thief some money. Some people in New York always carry money to give to a mugger. Don't fight. Your body is more valuable than your money. Alternatively, you may try to run away, shouting, screaming, etc. But never carry a knife or a gun or other weapons. If the criminal sees that you have a weapon he may use *his* weapon on you!

How to look after your valuables

You may want to make your own money belt. Use cotton material and

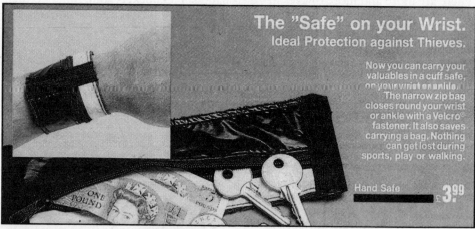

The "Safe" on your Wrist.
Ideal Protection against Thieves.

Now you can carry your valuables in a cuff safe, on your wrist or ankle. The narrow zip bag closes round your wrist or ankle with a Velcro® fastener. It also saves carrying a bag. Nothing can get lost during sports, play or walking.

Hand Safe £3.99

Shriek alarm scares off attackers! Like carrying a bodyguard in your handbag. Alarm's loud, shrill, hair-raising blast frightens would-be molesters, muggers, robbers! Pocket-size protector looks like a dainty perfume atomizer, yet a slight touch instantly triggers a piercing shriek that can be heard for blocks! Needs no batteries. Only 4½" long. Carry everywhere in handbag pocket; keep one by your bedside! You'll feel more secure!

Shriek Alarm £2.98

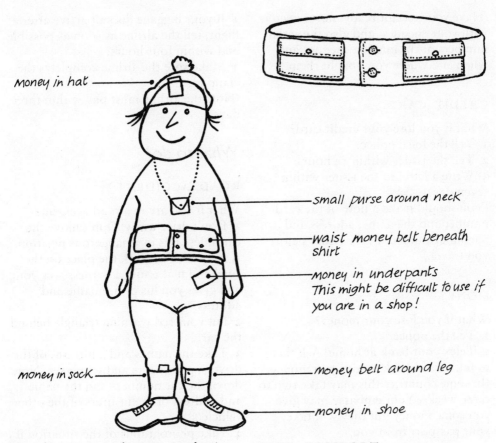

money in hat

small purse around neck

waist money belt beneath shirt

money in underpants
This might be difficult to use if you are in a shop!

money in sock

money belt around leg

money in shoe

keep the money and papers in plastic bags because you get hot and wet! Some people keep small valuables and money in their underpants, and there are plenty of other places where you can hide them if you want. However, if you are staying in a hotel, it is better to leave your passport, air tickets, traveller's cheques and money in the hotel safe.

Lost property

What should you do if you lose something, have an accident or become ill? Be prepared! Here are some sensible things to do. Learn them by heart so that you know what to do if an accident happens.

YOUR PASSPORT

What if you lose your passport?
1 Tell the local police.
2 Inform your nearest consul or embassy. They may be able to give you a temporary passport.
(You should keep a note of your passport number and the place and date of issue. You should really try to remember this information.)

TRAVELLER'S CHEQUES

What if you lose your traveller's cheques?
1 Tell the local police within 24 hours.
2 Tell the issuer, i.e. the bank, Thomas Cook, Bank of America, etc. within 24 hours.

(Have your receipt ready, never keep it with your cheques, and also the serial numbers of the missing cheques and when and where you bought them.)

CREDIT CARD

What if you lose your credit card?
1 Tell the local police.
2 Tell the issuer within 24 hours.
3 Write a letter to the issuer within seven days.
(You should make a note of the card number and the name, address and telephone number of the issuer before you travel.)

MONEY

What if you lose your money?
1 Tell the police.
2 Telex your bank at home. Ask them to tell a local bank to give you money.
(In some countries this may take two to three weeks. Your embassy may give you some money but they will take your passport from you.)

CAR DOCUMENTS

What if you lose your car documents?
Tell the local police and show them all the papers you have (if possible for the vehicle and for yourself).
(It is very helpful if you make photocopies of your papers before you leave. The police may give you temporary papers if they can see the photocopies.)

LUGGAGE

What if you lose your luggage?
1 If you lose your luggage in a hotel, tell the hotel management and the police.

2 If your luggage doesn't arrive after a flight, tell the airline as soon as possible and within four hours.
3 Make sure the airline completes the claim form.
(Note the airline must pay within three days.)

What to do?

ROAD ACCIDENT

What if you are in a road accident?
1 Don't drive away! Don't move the car unless it is in a dangerous position. If you move it, mark the place on the road and make sure a witness sees you and gives you his or her name and address.
2 Put your red warning triangle behind the car.
3 Take the names and addresses of the drivers, passengers and witnesses. Note down the car numbers and the name and address of the insurers of the other vehicle(s).
4 Take photographs of the situation if you can. Include photographs of the number plates. Note down what happened immediately if you can.
5 Tell your insurance company by letter within 24 hours.

POLICE!

What if the police stop you?
Pay what they ask but ask them to give you a receipt.

ARREST?

What if you are taken by the police?
Tell your nearest consulate or embassy.

ILLNESS

What if you become ill?
1 If it is an emergency, phone the emergency services. In Britain you dial 999 for an emergency. However, there must be a very serious reason!
2 If you are ill in a hotel or youth hostel, etc. the people who work there will contact the doctor for you. In Britain the doctor will come to you if you can't get to the surgery. Usually even ill people are expected to get to the surgery!
3 If you go to hospital, ask an official to inform your nearest consul or embassy. The consul or embassy will then inform your family, etc.
(Some countries may have an agreement with your country. Then you won't pay or, if you do, you will get your money back. In other countries you will not be looked after unless you can pay! So it is wise to have a good insurance.)

DEATH

What if one of your companions dies?
1 Tell your nearest consul or embassy.

2 Telephone or write to the relatives and/or friends.
★ Do you know your passport number, and when and where it was issued?!
★★ Have you ever had anything stolen while travelling in another country or at home?
★★ Tell your partner about any such experiences you have had.

How to look after a person who has been in an accident

★ Are you a calm person? How would you react in an emergency?
★ Imagine you are the first person to arrive at the scene of an accident. A man is still in his car, but he is not conscious. You can see he is breathing, and there is blood coming from his face. What should you do? What should you not do?
★★ Have you ever arrived on the scene soon after an accident? What did you feel? What did you do?

SHOCK

SHE'S NOT BREATHING

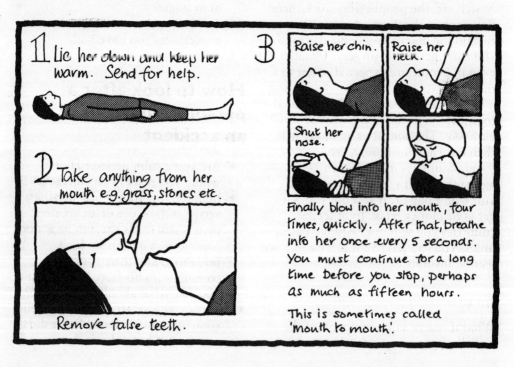

HER HEART'S NOT BEATING

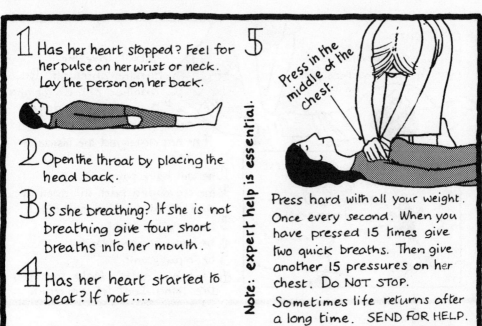

1 Has her heart stopped? Feel for her pulse on her wrist or neck. Lay the person on her back.

2 Open the throat by placing the head back.

3 Is she breathing? If she is not breathing give four short breaths into her mouth.

4 Has her heart started to beat? If not....

Note: expert help is essential.

5 Press in the middle of the chest.

Press hard with all your weight. Once every second. When you have pressed 15 times give two quick breaths. Then give another 15 pressures on her chest. Do NOT STOP.

Sometimes life returns after a long time. SEND FOR HELP.

BROKEN BONES

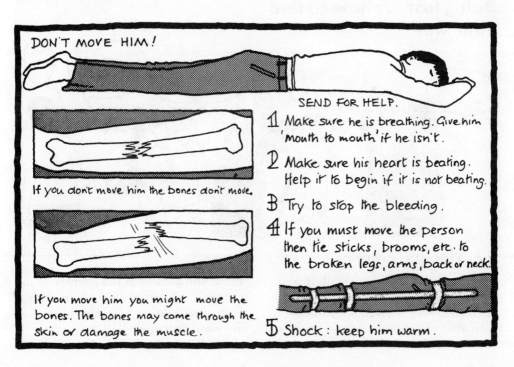

DON'T MOVE HIM!

If you don't move him the bones don't move.

If you move him you might move the bones. The bones may come through the skin or damage the muscle.

SEND FOR HELP.

1 Make sure he is breathing. Give him 'mouth to mouth' if he isn't.

2 Make sure his heart is beating. Help it to begin if it is not beating.

3 Try to stop the bleeding.

4 If you must move the person then tie sticks, brooms, etc. to the broken legs, arms, back or neck.

5 Shock: keep him warm.

CUTS AND BLEEDING

OPEN CUTS
Put a clean handkerchief over the cut and then press on it.

Don't take the handkerchief off. Put another one on top and then tie a bandage around it.

If he has damaged the inside of his body:
1 he will have pain
2 the damaged part will swell up and it will be blue and purple
3 he may be thirsty
4 he may cough blood
5 he may vomit
6 Keep him quiet. Make sure he is breathing. Don't let him drink.

Do not use a tourniquet unless he is bleeding to death!
Tourniquets are dangerous.

Being lost . . . how to find your way

I think it's that way!

I don't know and I feel sick.

Perhaps we should go back again.

Excuse me! I think we're lost.

So am I.

WALKING IN CIRCLES

It is almost impossible to walk in a straight line if you close your eyes! Challenge your friends! Some people turn after about three metres; some turn suddenly after about 10 metres.

Which do you do?
And if you are lost in the country or in a city you will probably walk in circles there as well unless you learn how to find your direction.

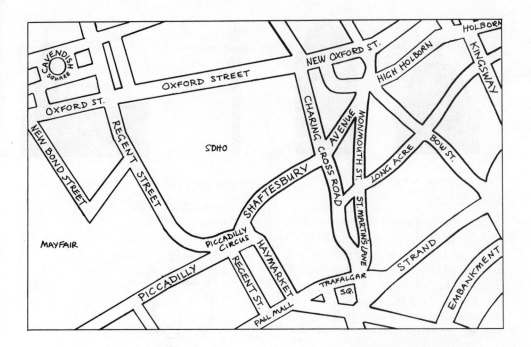

GET TO KNOW A CITY'S PATTERN

When you arrive in a new city, buy a map and try to remember the pattern and direction of the main streets.

Look at the street plan of London's West End for three minutes. Can you see the pattern that the following streets make: Oxford Street, Regent Street, Piccadilly, Piccadilly Circus, Charing Cross Road, Trafalgar Square, the Strand?

★ Now, close the book and try to draw the pattern and name the streets.

If you aren't successful, give yourself another three minutes. When you know the main pattern of streets you can fit the smaller streets into it.

★★ Is it possible to find a main pattern of streets in a part of your own city or town?

In many North American cities the pattern is there already as a chessboard of blocks.

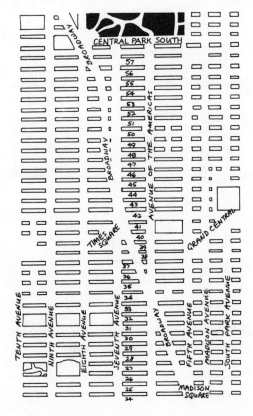

43

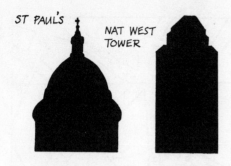

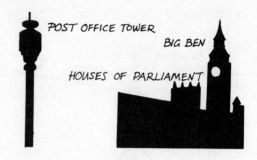

LEARN TO RECOGNISE TALL BUILDINGS

In London visitors should try to remember the following landmarks: St Paul's and the NatWest Tower which are east of the centre; the Post Office Tower which is north of the centre, and Big Ben and the Houses of Parliament which are south of the centre.

Can you use a compass?

Some drivers have a compass in their car. A compass is also useful for a walker in town and country. Of course, you must know your main direction. If you are at Holborn . . .

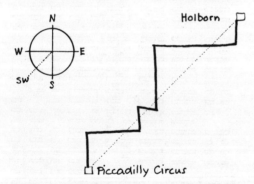

Piccadilly Circus, for example, is to the south-west. If you walk to the left of your main south-west direction then you must, later, walk back to the right, etc.

A COMPASS FROM A WATCH

★ You need a watch with hands, not a digital watch.

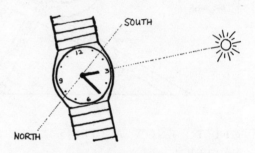

Point the hour hand at the sun. Imagine a line drawn between the hour hand and 12 o'clock. That line is pointing south and north. (This is according to Greenwich Mean Time.)
If it is British Summer Time (which is one hour later than Greenwich Mean Time) then imagine a line . . .

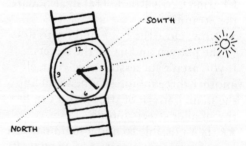

drawn between the hour hand and 1 o'clock. This idea with the watch works in the northern hemisphere of the world. Try it.

Your direction by the stars

It isn't difficult! Amaze your friends!
Here are two methods which help you
to find North.

Method 1

Look for a bright star low in the sky.
Look for a building or a tree which is
near the star. (You may have to move.)
Rest your head against something so
you are quite still.

After a few minutes the star will have
moved (because the earth is turning!).
If the star is going up you are looking
EAST.
If the star is going down you are
looking WEST.
If the star is moving to the right you are
looking SOUTH.
If the star is moving to the left you are
looking NORTH.

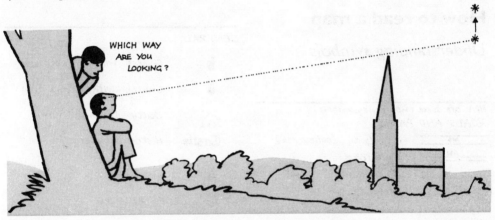

Method 2

Find the North Star if you are in the
northern hemisphere of the world. To
find the North Star you must first of all
find the Plough. Imagine a line joining
the two stars at the end of the Plough

and then continuing. This line shows
you where the North Star is.

In the southern hemisphere of the
world you must find the Southern
Cross. Then you can find North.

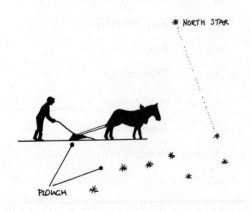

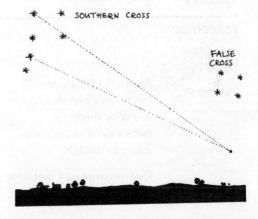

HOW TO USE THE SUN AND THE STARS

Your watch and the sun or the stars at night can give you the direction of North. However, to find a particular place you must know its direction from *where you are*. Then, as you walk along, you keep the star at the same angle to your route.

Keep the star on your left cheek!

How to read a map

Understanding symbols

Here are some important symbols:

ROADS AND PATHS

═══ m6 ═══	Motorway (called m6)
─── A31 ───	Main road
───────	Small road
- - - - - -	Footpath

RAILWAYS

───■───	Railway with a station

WATER

River joining a lake

Bridge crossing a river

VEGETATION

Wood: the trees are coniferous and keep their leaves in winter or deciduous and drop their leaves in winter.

Poor ground and moorland

GENERAL

⚲	Church with a tower
⚲	Church with a spire
⚔ 1066	Battle (example 1066)
Castle	Historical interest
Å	Camp site
🚐	Caravan site
P	Parking
i	Information
▲	Youth hostel
☎	Telephone
PC	Public convenience
☺	Bus station
⊻	Beautiful view
PO	Post office
PH/Inn	Public House
Sch	School
X	Picnic site

Hills

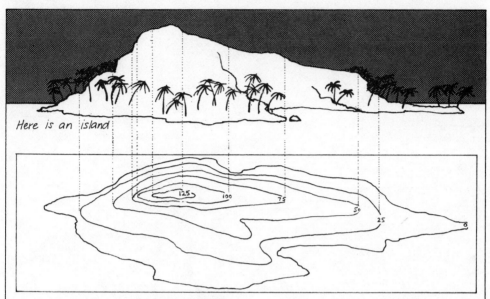

Here is an island

and here is a map of the island.

Each line is called a contour.
The first contour is 25' (feet)
or about 8 metres from the
level of the sea.

The highest part of the island
is 125' (feet), about 40 metres, above
the sea.
The steepest slope is on the
western end of the island.

Scale

All maps in Britain are being
changed from measurement by
miles to measurement by
kilometres. Today a useful
map for a walker or cyclist
is 1:50,000 or 1:25,000. This
means that 1cm on the map
equals 50,000 cm on the ground.
The map (1:50,000) is divided
into squares. Each square is
2cm and this equals 1 kilometre.

8 kilometres equal 5 miles

Grid reference

Where _is_ it exactly?

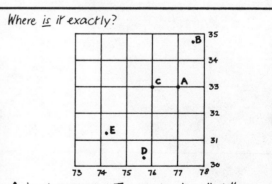

A is at 770330   The number is called the
B is at 775348   grid reference of the place.
Can you give the grid reference for C, D, E?

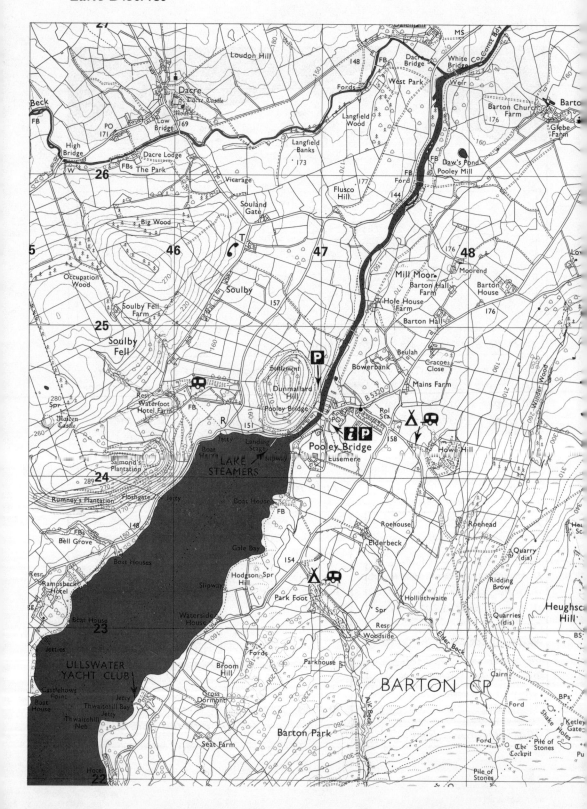

Look at the map of part of the Lake District opposite.

1 Can you give the grid reference of Dacre?

2 I am in Barton (grid reference 486265). How do I get to the pier for the lake steamers? Please give me directions and not a grid reference.

3 How many caravan sites are there on the map?

4 How many campsites are there?

5 Can I post a letter in Pooley Bridge?

6 Is it hilly country?

7 If I stand in Pooley Bridge and look over the River Eamont what can I see?

8 How many churches are there on the map?

9 Can you describe them?

10 Can the children in Pooley Bridge go to school there?

11 Where is the nearest school to Pooley Bridge?

12 Where is the nearest public telephone to West Park (grid reference 476266)? Please give me directions.

13 Which is the steepest road on the map (include small roads)?

14 Is there a railway near Pooley Bridge?

15 How can I get to Dacre? (I am at the Park Foot campsite, grid reference 469233.)

16 If I stand by the lake at Pooley Bridge, can I see Dacre?

17 Can I walk along a footpath from Hodgson Hill (grid reference 465233) to Pooley Bridge?

18 And where can I walk after Pooley Bridge?

19 Are there any old places of interest?

20 What can I see and where should I go?

21 Are there any mixed woods on the map?

22 How high above sea level is the lake?

23 Is Dacre higher above sea level than the stone circle called The Cockpit (grid reference 482222) or lower?

24 Describe what you can see if you walk from Pooley Bridge, past the church and up the hill to Roehead and on to The Cockpit.

25 How far is it from Barton to Park Foot campsite?

(The answers are on page 84.)

How to survive less common problems

Extreme cold

Over 20 people die in the mountains of Britain every year, many of them from the cold. The cold in a North American winter is well known. This section gives advice on how you can experience the beauty of the lonely and cold parts of these countries and come back to enjoy your memories!

BEFORE YOU START

Find out all you can about the route you want to take. Get good maps and guide books and talk to local people. Certainly listen to the weather forecast on the radio. However, expect the weather to change very rapidly. You may start off on a nice, bright day and by the afternoon be unable to stand up in powerful winds. Little streams may become rivers within an hour. And even in spring ice can cover rocks. Make sure you can use your compass and map easily and accurately. If you are ever in trouble you mustn't make a mistake.

Go with at least two other people. You need someone to stay with an injured person and someone to get help. Before you go, tell someone where you are going and the time you expect to arrive. When you arrive, let the people know that you have arrived, or a rescue team might be sent out to look for you! If you have no one to leave the information with, then leave the message on a note inside your car or some other place which is easy to find.

TAKE THE RIGHT EQUIPMENT

Half of all accidents are caused by poor clothing and poor footwear. Exposure to the cold and injuries to legs and ankles lead to 46% of all accidents.

IF ANYTHING GOES WRONG

Learn to know how quickly you can travel: a walker moves at about four km an hour. If you are going up hill add an extra half an hour for each 300 metres of ascent. You will take longer if you are carrying a heavy load.
Do not continue if something goes wrong:
a) If you are lost, stop and try to work out where you are with your map and compass.
b) If it is getting dark and one of your companions can't move then stay the night on the hills. (See the advice on keeping warm on pages 51 to 54.)
c) It is particularly important to keep injured people warm.
d) Get help. If you go for help you must remember the position of the injured person. Mark the position on a map and look carefully at the land around

you in order to remember the place. Try to remember your route to the nearest telephone. Mark the position of the accident on your map. Phone the police and give them the map reference, the time of the accident, the type of injury and how many people are left behind. (For how to signal for help see pages 60 to 61.)

A CHECKLIST FOR WALKERS

Are you wearing . . .
– brightly coloured wind and water proof clothing?
– suitable footwear?

Do you know . . .
– how to use your equipment?
– what time it gets dark?
– the International Mountain Distress Signal?

Have you left . . .
– information about where you are going with people who will miss you if you don't arrive?

Have you got . . .
– a map?
– a compass?
– a whistle?
– a torch?
– spare clothing (hat, gloves, scarf, etc.)?
– a watch?
– sandwiches and emergency food rations?
– first aid (lint for dressing cuts, bandages, plasters, aspirin, safety pins, antiseptic cream)?
– spare coins for telephoning?

If the answer to any of the above questions is 'No', the best advice to you is, don't go!

COLD KILLS

If someone is suffering from
hypothermia:
– they shiver
– they walk slowly and fall over things
– they speak with difficulty
– they can't see properly
– they are unreasonable, aggressive or
irritable

Drop five degrees and you are dead!

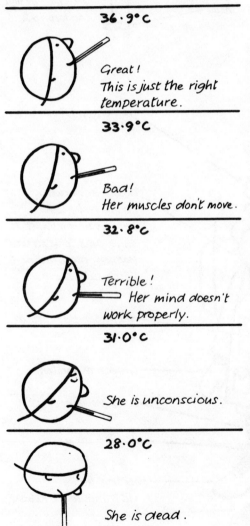

36·9°C

Great!
This is just the right
temperature.

33·9°C

Bad!
Her muscles don't move.

32·8°C

Terrible!
Her mind doesn't
work properly.

31·0°C

She is unconscious.

28·0°C

She is dead.

If someone is suffering from
hypothermia, you must stop. You must
get them out of the cold and the wind.
You must get into a shelter.
Hypothermia kills!
1 Put clothing, newspapers, branches,
etc. beneath them.
2 Cover them in as many clothes as
possible.
3 Put them in a sleeping bag if
possible. But first of all make the bag
warm . . . get in it yourself.
4 Human warmth is the best. You
must embrace the person with
hypothermia. If there are several
friends with you they must all gather
round the cold person.
5 Warm tea, etc. is good.
6 Sweets and candy are good because
they give immediate energy.

However,
NEVER put the person near a fire
NEVER give the person alcohol
NEVER give the person a hot water
bottle
NEVER rub the person
All these actions make freezing blood
rush from the skin to the heart.
THIS CAN KILL.

HOW YOUR BODY LOSES ITS HEAT

Low temperature, wind and wet are the killers. The wind carries away your body heat. So your body must make more heat . . . perhaps it can't.

Wet clothes can't hold the heat as well as dry clothes. Wet clothes lose heat 200 times faster than dry clothes. Therefore, low temperature, wind and wetness are the killers! You can get wet because you have got too hot; for example, you may have been wearing a plastic anorak and walking quickly.

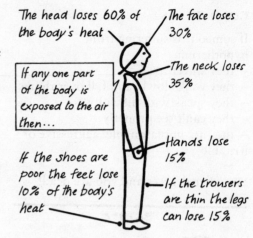

The head loses 60% of the body's heat

The face loses 30%

The neck loses 35%

If any one part of the body is exposed to the air then···

Hands lose 15%

If the trousers are thin the legs can lose 15%

If the shoes are poor the feet lose 10% of the body's heat

WHAT MUST A WELL-DRESSED WALKER WEAR?

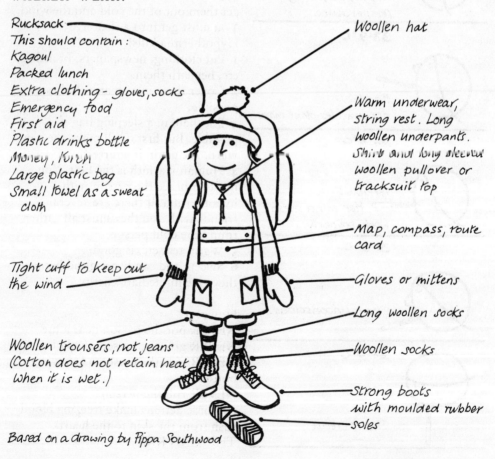

Rucksack
This should contain:
Kagoul
Packed lunch
Extra clothing - gloves, socks
Emergency food
First aid
Plastic drinks bottle
Money, torch
Large plastic bag
Small towel as a sweat
   cloth

Woollen hat

Warm underwear, string vest. Long woollen underpants. Shirt and long sleeved woollen pullover or tracksuit top

Map, compass, route card

Tight cuff to keep out the wind

Gloves or mittens

Long woollen socks

Woollen trousers, not jeans (Cotton does not retain heat when it is wet.)

Woollen socks

Strong boots with moulded rubber soles

Based on a drawing by Pippa Southwood

WHAT MATERIALS ARE GOOD IN COLD PLACES?

Wool is better than cotton. Wool doesn't soak up the wetness; it either falls off or fills the holes and helps to keep in body heat.

Cotton soaks up wetness, and wet cotton doesn't hold the heat. For example, wet jeans are dangerous in a very cold place.

Modern materials If you aren't moving and not giving off a lot of body heat, for example, in a sleeping bag, then use a material which totally prevents the air from passing through and therefore retains the heat of your body. If you are moving and perspiring then use material which allows the perspiration to get away from your body.

A sleeping bag should keep the heat in.

A kagoul should let the moisture out.

★★ Have you got all the necessary clothes for a week's walking in the hills (in the cold)?

FROSTBITE

When you shiver you burn sugar in your muscles and this makes you warm. However, when your body temperature drops too far, shivering doesn't help. The body stops the blood going to the hands and the feet. Your hands and feet will become very cold and they may even die . . . this is called frostbite.

Here is what you can do by yourself:
– don't wear anything which is too tight
– put your fingers under your armpits
– take your arms out of your sleeves and button up your coat

Is your belt too tight?

Are your shoes too tight?

fingers under the armpits

arms inside the coat

Here is what you can do with a friend:
– hug your friend
– sit with your toes under each other's armpits

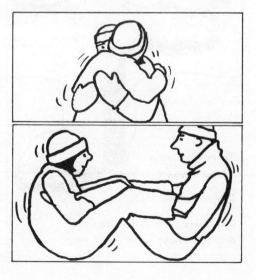

YOU MAY HAVE TO MAKE A SHELTER

If you make a shelter out of snow, the walls must be at least 60 cm thick. With walls like this you will remain quite warm! The temperature in a good snow shelter will not fall below −23°C even if the temperature outside is −50°C. And you can raise the temperature of the air inside with your body heat and with a small candle.

★★ Does it get very cold in winter in your country? Can it be dangerous? Do people die of the cold? What advice would you give to visitors?

★★ Tell your partner about any bad experience you have had because of the cold.

blocks of snow

tunnel

You can close the tunnel when you have gone into your igloo. However, you must leave a hole for air.

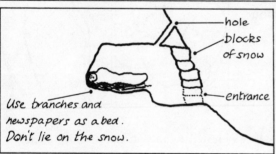

hole
blocks of snow
entrance

Use branches and newspapers as a bed. Don't lie on the snow.

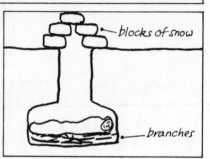

blocks of snow

branches

There is often a hollow around a tree.

Dig more snow out.

Cut some thin branches and use them as a bed.

branches

Never leave a car if it is stuck in the snow (unless you can see a house, etc.). Cover yourself as well as you can. If necessary tear the stuffing out of the seats and use that. You can run the engine for heat if the exhaust pipe is clear. Leave the window open a little bit. You must have good air!

How to stay alive in the desert

GENERAL PLANNING

1 You must tell the police, military or other responsible people where you are going.
2 Go with several vehicles.
3 Take a mirror and agree with your companions on signals and what they mean.

Light can be reflected by a mirror and be seen many miles away.

4 Have some flares with you. Let them off at night if you are in trouble.

5 Take a lot of water with you. Your car might break down so take extra water. For example for five days you should take 20 litres for each person.

If you are in trouble

Food isn't important in the desert, but water is! It is very important to keep the water in your body. The body tries to keep its temperature at 36.9°C. It cools itself by sweating, but you can't see that you are sweating because as soon as the water comes out of the skin it dries in the air.

The rules are:

1 Keep out of the sun during the day and rest. Work on your broken down car, crippled camel or walk for help, at night.
2 Wear light coloured clothing with long, loose, sleeves, and trousers. Wear a hat.
3 When you sweat you lose salt. You should make up for this by eating salt in pills or on your food.
4 If you leave your car, make large arrows with stones, etc. to show your direction.

Water in the desert

Sometimes birds can lead you to water. You might try and dig in dried up rivers and under plants or at the foot of a steep side of a sand dune.
But only do this work at night!

HOW LONG CAN YOU LIVE?

If you stay in the shade and don't walk . . .

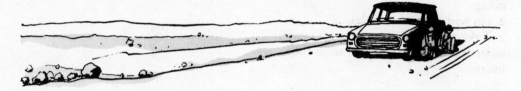

If you have   0 water and the temperature is 50°C you will live for   2½ days
     4 litres of water   50°C   3 days
     20 litres of water   50°C   4½ days

If you have   0 water and the temperature is 35°C you will live for   7 days
     4 litres of water   35°C   10 days
     20 litres of water   35°C   20 days

If you have   0 water and the temperature is 20°C you will live for   12 days
     4 litres of water   20°C   16½ days
     20 litres of water   20°C   36½ days

If you walk at night and rest in the shade during the day . . .

If you have
  0 water and the temperature is 50°C you will live for 1 day and walk 40 km
  4 litres of water   50°C   2½ days and walk 56 km
  10 litres of water   50°C   3½ days and walk 64 km

★★ Tell your partner what you would do if you had 10 litres of water left. You are in the desert, 50 km from the nearest town, the temperature is 25°C in the day, your landrover has broken down, and one of your two friends is ill!

Danger

IN SWAMPS AND QUICKSAND

Suddenly, your feet drop deep into the mud or into the sand! You are very frightened!! You pull up one leg and you sink deeper with the other leg! You are drowning!

Alternatively, throw yourself on your back. This keeps your face free.

Throw yourself forward! Roll your body from side to side until your feet are free. Then swim! If you have a backpack, take it off and push it underneath you.

ON ICE

If the ice breaks you must reach out over the ice and give a big kick with your legs. You must try to get your chest onto the ice. When you have found strong ice again you will be able to crawl onto it.

But . . . never go onto ice unless you are sure it is strong. Ice is usually stronger nearer to the land. However, it is usually weak around objects like trees, etc.

IN THE TENT

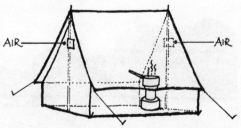

This tent is safe! Air passes through the tent – in one end and out the other. There is no danger of carbon monoxide.

⤳

57

This tent is not safe! The carbon monoxide increases. The flame of the cooker is yellow and not blue. The camper is sleeping . . . he may never wake up!

AVALANCHES

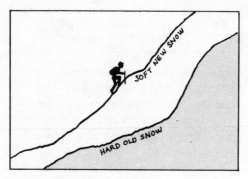

Avoid soft snow on a hillside. If the soft snow is on top of hard snow it is particularly dangerous. If an avalanche starts, what do you do? If you can hold

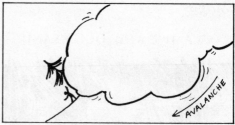

onto rocks or trees do so. If you can't hold onto anything you should try to 'swim' on your back; reach out and back with both your arms at once.

When the snow stops you must try to climb upwards. However, the snow may hold you very tightly. Try to keep your hand in front of your face, and keep your mouth shut. Don't move or you will use up your oxygen. You will have to wait until people find you with rescue dogs.

LIGHTNING

Lightning is dangerous in the following places:
Under oak trees

Under poplar trees

Under elm trees – these are the most dangerous

Safe places

It is fairly safe in a thick wood if all the trees are the same height.

Buildings or trees which stand by themselves are dangerous.

The electricity goes round the car and down into the earth.

Steep hillsides, rock faces and caves are also dangerous.

If you are in an open field you should lie flat on your stomach. Don't stand up!

If the thunder is only five seconds behind the lightning it is dangerous! Each five seconds indicates a distance of one mile between you and the lightning.

★ Are thunderstorms common in your country? Are people ever killed by lightning?
★★ Tell your partner about the most dramatic thunderstorm you have been in.

How to signal for help

IN A CAR

If you break down you can warn other motorists by raising the bonnet of your car and the boot. You should place a red, metal triangle fifty metres back along the road. If you haven't got a red triangle, put something else there which will attract attention: it could be a hub cap from your wheel or it could be a pile of branches.

IN THE MOUNTAINS

The International Mountain Distress Signal is six blasts on a whistle in one minute . . . then one minute of silence . . . then six more blasts. Continue until help comes. If this signal is heard by rescuers they should give three short blasts each minute, then a minute's silence. (You can use a torch in the same way.)

IN A BOAT

The morse code for help is

••• ━━━ •••.

If you have a radio you call, MAYDAY . . . MAYDAY . . . MAYDAY . . . then you give the name of your boat, your position, and the problem you have. Rockets always attract attention.

If you are in a small boat without any of these aids, then wave your arms or wave an oar . . . tie a white cloth to the end.

TO PILOTS

SOS

Write SOS on the ground in enormous letters.

The heliograph

If the sun is shining you can flash light at aeroplanes or at distant cars or other travellers. But you must *direct* the flash of light. This is how to do it with a tin lid.

If the sun is in front of you, polish the tin lid on both sides and put a hole through the middle. Look at the aeroplane (distant car, etc.) through the hole. The sun will shine through the hole and will make a small circle of light on your face. You will see this circle in the mirror of the tin lid. Now, move (tilt) the lid until this circle of light disappears. You are now flashing a signal at the aeroplane.

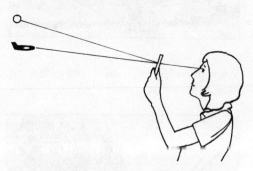

If the sun is above you, look at the aeroplane through the hole. The sun will shine through it and will make a small circle of light on your hand. Now tilt the lid until this circle of light disappears. You are now flashing a signal at the aeroplane.

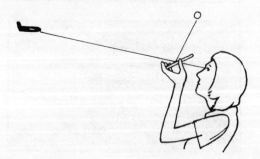

This is how to do it if you have a piece of glass or a mirror. Hold out your left hand towards the plane. Open your fingers a little bit so that you can see the plane. Tilt the mirror until the light of the sun is on your fingers. Then the aeroplane will see the light.

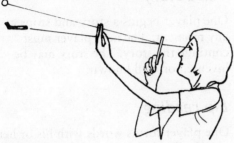

With a fire

A fire will attract attention. The best signal for an aeroplane is three fires in an equilateral triangle. This means SOS, and is understood by pilots throughout the world.

★★ Have you ever had to signal for help? What happened?
★★ Imagine you are the only survivor after your ship has sunk. You have swum to a small island, and are quite safe. You are not even hungry, but you don't want to stay there for ever. What would you do?

Games for boring moments

Sometimes when you are travelling you may have to wait a long time without being able to move or without anything to do:
– if your flight is delayed by several hours
– if your car breaks down and you have to wait a long time for the mechanic to come
– if you are hitching and there is no traffic
– if you are on a long train journey, going through boring countryside and have finished your book.
You may feel bored! It can be a good idea to play games to help the time pass more quickly, without feeling too bored. Some of these games may be very useful to you one day!

Did you see that car?

This game tests your memory. The first player points at something outside the car. Then he or she says, for example, 'Did you see that car?' The next player must repeat the sentence and add more information to it, for example, 'Did you see that red car?' And the next player must continue by repeating what has been said and then adding more information.
   The information must be true. If it isn't true and if all the players agree that it isn't the game is over. Or you can allow people to invent things providing they might be true!

Find your letters to spell your word

A player thinks of a four letter word

and writes it down without showing it to the others. Then he or she must see and point to objects whose names contain the letters of the word. For example, if I write down GATE, I can cross off each letter if I see the following objects . . . *garage*, *path*, *light*, *fence*.

The other player(s) have to guess which word you have chosen.

I'm hiding

One player imagines that he or she is hiding at home or in a place everyone knows. The others try to find out where he or she is hiding. They have 20 questions.

How many in one minute?

Decide on an object or type of person which is very common where you are. For example, in an airport you might choose people in uniform, or children under five, or people wearing glasses. Then try to find as many examples as possible of the object or type of person in one minute.

Traffic police: who has the sharpest eyes?

Look for dangerous behaviour! If a pedestrian, or driver (or animal) does anything foolish, note it down.

Guessing time and distance

One player looks at a watch. The others close their eyes. The player with the watch tells the others when the minute is starting. The others have to guess when the minute has passed. Each player says, NOW, when he or she thinks the minute is complete.

Alternatively, the passengers in a car close their eyes. The driver tells them when a new kilometre is beginning. The passengers try to guess when the kilometre is complete.

Tell a story

One player begins a story and stops at any moment. The next player must continue the story. The story may be invented or well known.

Lip reading

One player forms words with his or her mouth silently. The other players try to guess what he or she is saying. The game can be restricted, for example, to names, numbers or describing something nearby.

How to plan a holiday in Britain

What do you really want?

The questions below might help you to decide what sort of holiday you would like to have in Britain.

Do you like to relax and do very little on holiday?
In that case see pages 65 and 68.

Do you like history?
There is a lot for you to do in Britain! See page 67.

Do you like music, theatre, dance and art?
Britain is a rich country for the arts. See page 64.

Do you want to meet British people?
Here are some good ways of getting to know them . . . see page 69.

Do you want to learn a new hobby?
See page 70.

Do you like shopping and city life?
See page 64.

Are you a sportswoman or a sportsman?
See page 70.

And what about walking and looking at nature?
See page 66.

How about a free holiday?!
See page 73.

EDINBURGH

LONDON

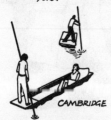

YORK

CAMBRIDGE

Holidays in a city

Do you like shopping? Do you want to go to the theatre, to the cinema, to night clubs and discotheques, to a variety of restaurants? If so, you must stay in a city!

The two great holiday cities are Edinburgh and London. But there are other smaller cities you might consider: York, Chester, Oxford, Cambridge, Warwick and Bath are all excellent for holidays. They are big enough to offer a variety of entertainment, restaurants and fascinating places to visit. Note, too, the international festivals of art and music in York, Bath and Edinburgh. All of these cities have ancient historical buildings and interesting museums. Furthermore, these cities are all surrounded by lovely countryside.

During the festivals there are entertainers in the street as well as in the theatre. Here is Annie Stainer, Britain's greatest mime artist, performing in St Giles Cathedral in Edinburgh and her husband Reg with his Suitcase Circus for Children during the Edinburgh Festival.

OXFORD

WARWICK

BATH

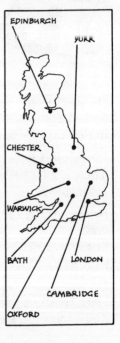

Holidays by the sea

warm clothes with you. If you like fishing, you will enjoy fishing from beaches, piers and motor boats. You will be sure of a good catch!

Of course some beaches in Britain are crowded in the summer. However, even in the warmest weather there are many miles of sandy beach where you can sit and dream by yourself . . . if that is what you want. If you like long, sandy beaches, go to Wales or the North-East coast (Northumbria). In the West country there are 650 miles of magnificent beaches, headlands and cliffs, particularly in Devon and Cornwall. The sea around the British coast is never very warm for swimming, but it is clear. If you are used to swimming in warm seas you will probably feel very cold in the British sea! However, you can sit and watch British people and North Europeans swimming and enjoying themselves!

There can be weeks of sunny weather in Britain. On the other hand the weather can change rapidly; the morning might be fine and sunny and the afternoon cool and the evening fine again. So if you go to the beach, take

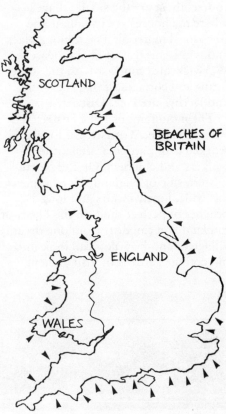

65

The green and pleasant land

If you arrive in Britain by air you will see below you a pattern of green fields and woods. The grass is rich, there are many mature trees and hedgerows, small woods, hills and valleys filled with wild flowers and birds. And, of course, there are the small villages where the houses are usually made from local material. The famous black and white cottages of Shakespeare's Warwickshire contrast with the stone farms and cottages of the Yorkshire and Derbyshire Peak District.

The mountainous Lake District where the poet Wordsworth lived and worked is of particular delight for walkers and climbers. On the North-Eastern side of England, Northumbria has wide, lonely moors and long beaches of perfect sand. In the Heart of England you can drift from one dreamy village to another. You can look into old cottage gardens or visit ancient castles and churches. In the West Country, apart from the miles of magnificent beaches, there are wooded valleys leading up to high, wild, and lonely countryside which is perfect for independent minded walkers.

And in Britain as a whole there are over 160,000 km of footpaths, which means that you don't need to look at the countryside from the road but you can walk as far as you want and really enjoy the beauty of the country.

A country full of history

Britain must be one of the richest countries in the world for buildings and sites of historical interest.

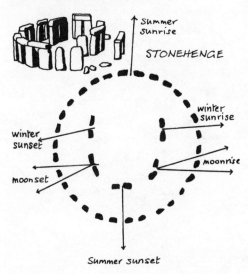

Stonehenge was built in about 1800 BC. It was probably used as a giant calculating machine to calculate the position of sunrise and sunset at different times of the year; it may also have been used to calculate the position of the stars.

Hadrian's Wall was built by the Romans in 128 AD to keep wild tribes of people in the North. There are many other Roman remains in Britain, for example, baths in Bath, and remains of houses and castle walls in York.

The oldest part of Haddon Hall in Derbyshire was built in the eleventh century. Then, during the next 500 years the owners added on new parts to the building. It is, therefore, a wonderful collection of different periods of medieval architecture. There is also a story of love! Dorothy Vernon ran away from here in 1563 to marry her lover. (She eloped during the evening of her sister's wedding dance. Her lover was waiting for her outside the Hall with horses.) In many old houses and castles in Britain there are stories of romance and, of course, ghosts.

A small picture from one of the fifteenth century windows.

A stone carving from the outside of the Minster.

York Minster is one of many wonderful medieval churches in England. The size of the Minster is impressive but the details of the sculpture and the stained glass windows also give a lot of pleasure.

The National Trust owns many houses, castles and areas of countryside in Britain which are usually open to the public. Look out for this sign:

STYAL CAR PARK

A lazy canal holiday

There are 4,800 km of rivers and canals in Britain. Why not hire a boat and pass slowly through the fields and woods, the hills and towns of England? You can go down the valley of the Thames; you can cross the Pennine hills by the Leeds and Liverpool canal. You don't need to be a sailor! You will be taught all you need to know in a few minutes.

You can hire a boat which is big enough for two people or you might like to hire a 20 metre boat which is big enough for 12 people. In the cabin you will find a cooker and a freezer and all the facilities you need. The cost of hiring a boat for four people for one week is about £180.

POST CARD

CORRESPONDENCE

August 17th

Dear Katy,

We're having a wonderful holiday on a barge. Everything is so quiet and beautiful. We hope you are having a good time as well.

Love Rachel

Katy

12 L

Manc

N

© 1979 THE SUTCLIFFE GALLERY WHITBY
by agreement with Whitby Literary and Philosophical Society

THIS IS A JAYSCALE REPRODUCTION
Printed by John S. Speight Ltd., Guiseley, Nr. Leeds

DRINKINGS
A group of haymakers, probably at Lealholm Hall Farm. Amongst them are Alice Chambers, Tailor Bill Readman and Willie Wren. By Frank Meadow Sutcliffe.
20-6B

seat table cupboards   cupboard
COCKPIT   CABIN   COCKPIT
       SALOON   SHOWER   WC
              seat/bed   bed

A FEW OF THE WATERWAYS OF BRITAIN

Holiday centres

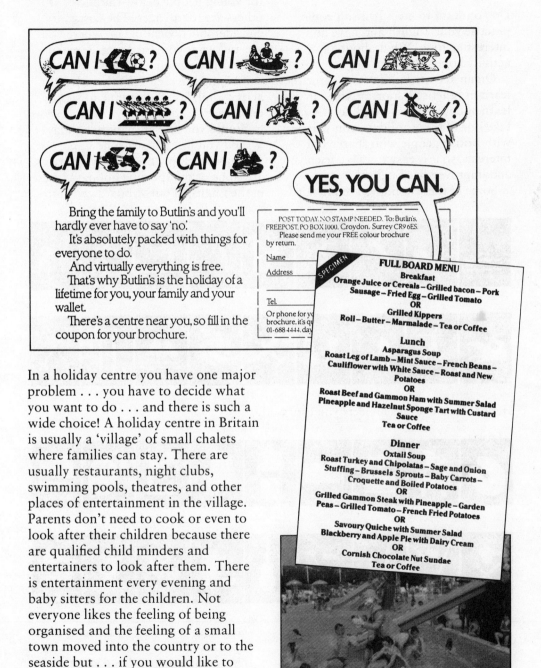

CAN I ⚽ ? CAN I 🚣 ? CAN I 🎱 ?

CAN I 💃 ? CAN I 🎠 ? CAN I ⛵ ?

CAN I 🛼 ? CAN I 🏎 ? **YES, YOU CAN.**

Bring the family to Butlin's and you'll hardly ever have to say 'no.'

It's absolutely packed with things for everyone to do.

And virtually everything is free.

That's why Butlin's is the holiday of a lifetime for you, your family and your wallet.

There's a centre near you, so fill in the coupon for your brochure.

POST TODAY. NO STAMP NEEDED. To: Butlin's, FREEPOST. PO BOX 1000. Croydon. Surrey CR9 6ES.
Please send me your FREE colour brochure by return.

Name

Address

Tel.

Or phone for yo
brochure. it's qu
01-688 4444. day

FULL BOARD MENU

SPECIMEN

Breakfast
Orange Juice or Cereals – Grilled bacon – Pork
Sausage – Fried Egg – Grilled Tomato
OR
Grilled Kippers
Roll – Butter – Marmalade – Tea or Coffee

Lunch
Asparagus Soup
Roast Leg of Lamb – Mint Sauce – French Beans –
Cauliflower with White Sauce – Roast and New
Potatoes
OR
Roast Beef and Gammon Ham with Summer Salad
Pineapple and Hazelnut Sponge Tart with Custard
Sauce
Tea or Coffee

Dinner
Oxtail Soup
Roast Turkey and Chipolatas – Sage and Onion
Stuffing – Brussels Sprouts – Baby Carrots –
Croquette and Boiled Potatoes
OR
Grilled Gammon Steak with Pineapple – Garden
Peas – Grilled Tomato – French Fried Potatoes
OR
Savoury Quiche with Summer Salad
Blackberry and Apple Pie with Dairy Cream
OR
Cornish Chocolate Nut Sundae
Tea or Coffee

In a holiday centre you have one major problem . . . you have to decide what you want to do . . . and there is such a wide choice! A holiday centre in Britain is usually a 'village' of small chalets where families can stay. There are usually restaurants, night clubs, swimming pools, theatres, and other places of entertainment in the village. Parents don't need to cook or even to look after their children because there are qualified child minders and entertainers to look after them. There is entertainment every evening and baby sitters for the children. Not everyone likes the feeling of being organised and the feeling of a small town moved into the country or to the seaside but . . . if you would like to meet a lot of British people then you might consider going to a holiday centre.

Activity holidays

Do you want to meet British people, practise your English and have an interesting time? What about an activity holiday?

On an activity holiday you can either learn or practise a sport or you can learn about a subject you like. If you take one of these holidays you will be with British people who share your interests, so it is easy to make friends and improve your English!

Some of these holidays are intended for young people below the age of 18, others are for all ages. The costs vary considerably depending on where you are and what you are doing. Some of these organisations specialise in combining learning English with an activity holiday. (See useful addresses on page 77.)

Would you like an activity holiday? Would you like to learn a new sport or perhaps develop a new hobby? Here are some of the sporting holidays listed in the English Tourist Board brochure:

Here are some of the subjects you can study:

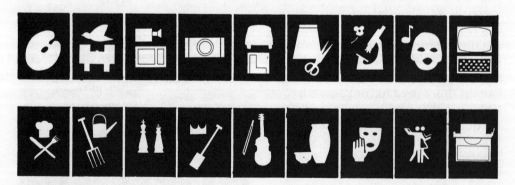

★ How many of these sports and activities are offered in the advertisements which follow?

★★ It is often a good idea to discuss your ideas with a friend. Friends usually know if you are dreaming or being serious! Tell a friend what you would like to do and see what he or she thinks of your idea! And, in any case, why not write to the organisations and see if you can get their up-to-date information?

PGL–Outstandingly different holidays for everyone

With over 26 years' experience, PGL now offer you the widest choice and the biggest range of very different holidays for all the family.

Safe. Supervised. Fun. Children's activities 6-12, Teenage adventure 13-18, Sports coaching 7-21, Family activities – in centres all around the UK.

PGL – any other holiday is drab in comparison. Find out more. Send for our action-packed brochures.

- SAILING ● CANOEING
- RIDING ● CRUISING
- ARTS & CRAFTS
- BACKPACKING
- RIFLESHOOTING
- FISHING ● TENNIS
- ORIENTEERING
- ARCHERY ● SOCCER
- WINDSURFING
- MULTISPORTS
- CAMPING ● TOURING
- CITY TOURS
- ABSEILING
- SWIMMING

Cycling Plus

The Welsh borderlands around Monmouth are well-known for their glorious scenery, historic towns and majestic ruined castles. Our 3 day cycling programme will explore many of these attractions, travelling at a leisurely pace along country lanes through the rolling countryside. We provide adjustable touring cycles to suit children and adults, capes for wet weather and a PGL courier who will be your companion, guide and travelling mechanic.

The week's programme also includes 2 days enjoying the varied range of activities back at the school in Monmouth and 1 free day to relax completely or travel by car to further points of interest beyond the cyclist's reach.

(Reproduced by kind permission of PGL Adventure Holidays)

Canoeing Plus

The River Wye — Britain's most
famous salmon river — is one of the
best rivers in the UK for introducing
canoe cruising. It is a gentle river,
flowing through beautiful scenery,
yet has sufficient stretches of fast water
to ensure that the canoeing is always
interesting. And at Symonds Yat
there's the best rapid on the lower
river to provide extra exhilaration.
All canoeing is downstream, so the
current can assist the less energetic
paddlers, and takes place under the
expert eye of PGL instructors. We use
single and double kayaks and open
Canadian canoes.

SPECIAL BONUS

Everyone on our Super-Choice
holiday, from seven years upwards,
will have the fantastic opportunity to
experience the exhilaration of gliding
on an introductory flight arranged for
us by The Cotswold Gliding Club at
special discount rates. Full details
and prices will be available at the
holiday centre.

Riding Plus

Puts the emphasis on trekking in the
hills around Denbigh. It's one of the
best ways to see the surrounding
countryside on a programme aimed
at the less experienced, but that
everyone can enjoy. 3 days are spent
on the riding programme.

The remaining 3 days consist of:

1 day of on-site activities back at
Howell's School.

1 day guided hill-walk.

1 free day.

(Reproduced by kind permission of PGL Adventure Holidays)

Millfield Village of Education

English for Foreigners (Adults)

1m, 2m, 3m and 4m. Four courses.
Fee: £49.00
For adults who wish coaching and practice in various aspects of English, especially the spoken language (and with particular reference to colloquial speech).

These courses take place in the mornings only, affording an opportunity for foreign adults to enjoy recreational courses in the afternoons. Tutors will be drawn, in the main, from Millfield's own long established Foreigners' English Department, which employs those with many years' experience of teaching people from abroad, or of teaching abroad themselves.

Watercolour Painting

1a, 2a, 3a, and 4a. Four courses.
Fee: £39.00
Although these courses are structured primarily for beginners of 12 years and over (and adults, of course) in this most attractive art form, anybody with some experience is always welcome. Everybody will find something to suit their capabilities. With watercolour painting, as with so many other art media, there is always more to learn, more to enjoy. While we'll concentrate, obviously, on the special skills of painting in colour wash and tone variation, we'll take a close look at the techniques of perspective and proportion. We'll do studio and outdoor work – especially landscape. The fee covers: cost of all materials, and the course centre will be one of the school's Art Studios. To ensure that you will get the most from it, each course takes relatively few members.
I.R. Read, Dip.A.D.,A.T.C., Head of Art Department, Millfield.

English for Foreigners (Children)

Six week residential course for foreign boys and girls wishing to learn English. 14th July to 23rd August.

How to have a free holiday!

Free? Nothing is free in life! You have to work! But you don't pay for your stay and you do interesting things and get to know British people. Work includes: archaeology, work with children, work with disabled people, conservation work (making footpaths, making places for children to play, cleaning out old canals and ponds), working in hotels and holiday camps, farm work, etc.

If you are interested, then why not write to the Central Bureau for Educational Visits and Exchanges (address on page 77). The most useful book they publish is *Working Holidays*. This lists many working holidays in Britain and other countries including Australia and the United States. Note: not every holiday is totally free. In most cases you have to pay for your journey and in some cases you are asked to contribute towards the cost of your food.

Where are you going to stay?

Which of these are important to you?
1 Cost
2 Comfort (room, bed, bathroom)
3 Whether everything is done for you (room cleaned, meals cooked, etc.)
4 Meals available
5 Convenience (telephone, shops, television, etc.)

6 Meeting British people
If you know what you want then it will help you to decide whether you want to: camp, stay in a caravan, stay in a Youth Hostel, rent a holiday cottage, stay in 'bed and breakfasts', stay in a farmhouse or in hotels. Or perhaps you would like to stay with a British family.

Holiday cottages

If you want to be free to come and go when you wish and to eat when you wish, then a holiday cottage might be the answer. There are holiday cottages, flats and chalets in the country and by the sea which you can rent for a week or longer. The cost depends on where the cottage is, how many people can sleep in it and which part of the year you want it for.

COUNTRY COTTAGE AGENCY

Dept ETB, Lansdowne Place, 17 Holdenhurst Road, Bournemouth, Dorset BH8 8EH.
(0202) 295006 (24-hr dial-a-brochure); (0202) 25545 (Admin/bookings). Telex 418228. Prestel 2221360.

Over 200 personally inspected carefully selected properties in both country and coastal locations, sleeping 2-12 people, throughout many areas of England including Cotswolds, Kent, Sussex, Hampshire, New Forest, Dorset, Devon, Somerset, Cornwall. Available all year. Short Breaks out of season. All prices include VAT. Send for free colour brochure.

NO. OF PEOPLE ACCOMMODATED	LOWEST STARTING PRICE PER PROPERTY PER WEEK (INC. VAT)	
	LOW SEASON	HIGH SEASON
2	£54	£106
2-4	£63	£126
4-6	£69	£138
6-8	£81	£162
8-10	£93	£295
10-12	£105	£324

Farmhouse holidays

BETWS FAWR FARM: Criccieth
A working farm with beef and sheep on 170 acres, ideally situated on the Lleyn Peninsula for access to the sea and mountains of Snowdonia. Riding, fishing and shooting available.

ABERMEURIG MANSION: Lampeter
Abermeurig is a Georgian mansion situated on the banks of the River Aeron. Private shooting and fishing available on the farm. Enjoy a glass of wine with excellent farmhouse fare.

LOWER GWESTYDD FARM: Newtown
A 17th century black and white farmhouse, with a wealth of oak beams. Home produced beef, lamb and chicken together with home-grown fruit and vegetables are served in season. Fishing, golf and pony trekking available nearby.

MAESGWYN FARM: Ruthin
Maesgwyn is a 130 acre sheep and dairy farm situated in wild, unspoilt hill country between the market towns of Ruthin, Bala and Corwen. Fishing and sailing available nearby at Llyn Brenig.

BYRDIR FARM: Barmouth
Byrdir is a 40 acre Welsh beef and sheep farm. It is set in the heart of Snowdonia with beautiful views of Cardigan Bay and Rhinog Mountains, golf, fishing, swimming and pony trekking. Children welcome

PENTRE FARM: Lampeter
A 300 acre dairy and sheep farm situated in an elevated position overlooking the Vale of Teifi. There is fishing on the River Teifi and rough shooting on farmland.

Get away from the busy rush and noise of city life! Spend a week or two in a farmhouse: live the life of the country, enjoy the fields, the woods and the healthy, clean air. You and your friends or your family will enjoy the friendly care of the farmer and his family. You will not only have the interesting life of the farm to watch but the endless variety of the country. Many farms can arrange fishing or riding for you. Some farms give you bed and breakfast only, others give you all your meals.

Bed and breakfast

A 'Bed and Breakfast' is a private house where there are a few spare rooms for guests. Breakfast is always included in the price. There are bed and breakfasts in every town and village in Britain. You don't usually have to book in advance . . . you just stop at one which attracts you. Bed and breakfast is usually good and cheap! Prices may be as low as £6 per night per person. If you stay in bed and breakfasts you can meet a lot of British people and see different British homes. You can easily recognise a bed and breakfast guest house by a sign like this one . . .

Youth hostels

Both young and old people use the 280 Youth Hostels in England and Wales. If you want to stay in a Youth Hostel during the summer and in a popular place then you should write and book your place. It costs about £3.50 a night and £1.50 for breakfast or dinner. For further information write to YHA headquarters. See useful addresses on page 78.

Camping and caravanning

There are many camping and caravanning sites where you can stay in Britain. Some of them are large and have excellent facilities (toilets, washrooms, shops and cafés). There are also many campsites on small farms where you may have the advantage of being on a small site, perhaps in beautiful country far from towns and cars and noise. To find out more information about camping see useful addresses on page 78.

(Reproduced by kind permission of PGL Adventure Holidays).

Hotels

British hotels are graded according to quality. A five star hotel is a top quality hotel (and charges top prices!). However, many of the smaller hotels, particularly those in the smaller towns may not have a star but are very comfortable and pleasant to stay in. The more expensive hotels outside London cost at least £30 per night including breakfast for two people. Inexpensive hotels can cost between £10 and £20 per night. Hotels in London usually cost considerably more.

Families

Would you like to stay with a family? You would certainly practise your English and you would learn a lot about life in a British family home. What sort of family would you like to stay with, where and for how long? The British Tourist Board publishes the addresses of organisations which help you to find where to stay. The publication is called *Meet the British*.

Useful addresses

General

Ask these organisations for information on all their publications, then you can send for the ones you need.

British Tourist Authority, Queen's House, 64 St James's Street, London SW1A 1NF (Tel. 01 730 3488)

English Tourist Board, Thames Tower, Black's Road, Hammersmith, London W6 9EL

Wales Tourist Board, Brunel House, 2 Fitzalan Road, Cardiff CF2 1UY

Scottish Tourist Board, 23 Ravelston Terrace, Edinburgh EH4 3EU

Northern Ireland Tourist Board, River House, 48 High Street, Belfast BT1 2DS

Note: many of the bigger towns and cities have tourist information centres. You could try writing to: Tourist Information Service, The Town Hall (town or city).

Activity holidays for adults and young adults

Central Bureau for Educational Visits and Exchanges, Seymour Mews House, Seymour Mews, London W1H 9PE (They publish *Young Visitors to Britain*. It is specially for young people and gives information on the variety of ways of making contact with people and having an interesting time in Britain through travel, working holidays, activity holidays, educational visits, etc.)

Hobby and Leisure Holidays, Compton House, St Peter's Road, Bournemouth, Dorset BH1 2NT

Millfield Village of Education, Street, Somerset BA16 0YD

National Institute of Adult Education, 52–54 High Holborn, London WC1 (They publish lists of information on special courses in Britain.)

PGL Adventure Ltd, Station Street, Ross-on-Wye, Herefordshire HR9 7AH

Vacation Work, 9 Park End Street, Oxford (They publish, *Summer Jobs in Britain* and *Summer Employment Directory of the USA*.)

Holiday cottages

Taylings Holiday Cottages, 14 High Street, Godalming, Surrey (They publish a book containing over 1,000 addresses of holiday accommodation. The selection includes Georgian mansions, thirteenth century thatched cottages and castles!)

Canal holidays

Eurocruisers, Lloyds Bank Chambers, High Street, Haslemere, Surrey GU27 1JE (They publish a complete list of boat hire operators.)

Holiday centres

They advertise in the tourist magazines. However, you might like to write to one of the biggest and ask about their holidays:

Butlins Holidays Ltd, Bognor Regis, W. Sussex PO21 1JJ

Youth hostels

YHA Headquarters, Trevelyan House, 8 St Stephen's Hill, St Albans, Herts (Or write to the YHA in your own country who will be able to give you information on Youth Hostels in any country in the world.)

Camping and caravanning

Camping Club of Great Britain and Ireland, 11 Lower Grosvenor Place, London SW1W 0EY (For a small fee you can join the Camping Club. Their annual guide contains information on 2,000 sites in Britain and Ireland.)

Hotels

In most big cities there are information services which can let you know about hotels and costs within their city limits. Write to: Tourist Information Service, The Town Hall (name of the town or city) and your letters should reach the right people.

Families

The British Tourist Authority publishes the addresses of organisations which will help you to find where to stay. The publication is called *Meet the British*.

How to understand holiday brochures

If you decide to have a holiday in Britain or the United States then you may get a holiday brochure in English. (Send for some from the Tourist Offices in your country or write to one of the addresses on pages 77 and 78.) You are probably very good at reading holiday brochures in your own language! Most holiday brochures are similar. The writer wants to persuade you that the holiday is wonderful and just what you want. But is it what you want? What do you want from a holiday? And just what is the writer saying?

Florida

Look at the text and the pictures about Florida.

★ What can you do in Florida if you go there on holiday? See if you can list five main ideas.

FLORIDA

Florida conjures pictures of sandy beaches, lush palm trees and glorious sunshine, perfect ingredients for the sun-seeking holidaymaker; however, there is much, much more.

Orlando and the Central Florida region offer what is probably the most concentrated area of Theme Parks in the world, providing entertainment for every member of the family.

There's world-famous Walt Disney World, Sea World, Circus World, Wet n' Wild, Busch Gardens and the incredible new Disney Complex, E.P.C.O.T., a fascinating

insight into the world of tomorrow.

The contrasting coastal resorts of Miami Beach and Fort Lauderdale on the East Coast, and Clearwater Beach and St. Petersburg Beach on the West are ideal locations for either a stay-put holiday, or to combine as a two-centre arrangement with Orlando.

The primaeval beauty of the Everglades and the contemporary technology of the Kennedy Space Centre are just two more of the fascinating attractions not to be missed. Whatever your taste, America's number 1 Sunshine State of Florida will offer you the opportunity to enjoy the holiday of a lifetime.

ORLANDO

Mention Orlando and most people think immediately of Walt Disney World, the fun-filled fantasy kingdom of that master 'imagineer' Walt Disney. Now Central Florida is home to the latest Disney creation, the 1,000 million dollar complex of E.P.C.O.T. Twice the size of Walt Disney World, the Experimental Prototype City Of Tomorrow, is destined to become the number one tourist attraction in the United States and should not be missed by anyone visiting Florida.

Apart from the obvious attraction of the Disney showcase, Central Florida has a great deal to offer including Sea World, Cypress Gardens, Barnum and Bailey's Circus World, the Kennedy Space Centre and much much more. Add to this the famous beach resorts, year round sunshine and Airplan's range of top value accommodation, and it's not difficult to understand why this area is so popular with visitors.

HOLLYWOOD BEACH

The fashionable resort of Hollywood Beach is located in an idyllic setting between Miami Beach and Fort Lauderdale. The picturesque inland Inter-Coastal Waterways are fronted by the magnificent stretch of sandy Hollywood Beach, where you will be able to combine a mixture of leisurely sun-bathing with a wide range of water sport activities.

MIAMI BEACH

The world-famous resort, with its twelve miles of golden sands, offers a multitude of activities for all the family. Connected to the mainland by a series of causeways, the "island" stretches from South Miami Beach with its array of glittering hotels, through the exclusive area of Bal Harbour to Northern Sunny Isles. The resort enjoys a semi-tropical climate, ideal for taking home that famous "Florida Tan".

(From an American Airplan brochure)

If you have found five main ideas then you have succeeded. Congratulations! Some of the adjectives don't add any useful information and some do. For example, 'sandy' tells us that the beaches aren't stony . . . so that is useful information; 'glorious' doesn't add any useful information. Can you find another example of a useful adjective and another of a useless adjective in the text? List these 'useless' adjectives and learn to recognise them quickly. They tell you nothing except that the writer (or the speaker) is trying to persuade you to do something!

Brochure writers like to list facts or opinions so that they persuade us to go to a particular place. How many lists can you find in this text?

The five (or more) main ideas you found are the five things which the writer thinks that you think are important! Do you think these things are important for you? If not, which five things would you demand for your holiday? The writer, very understandably, doesn't criticise Florida. Can you imagine any disadvantages for you if you went on holiday there?

Can you read costs?

Can you work out hotel and travel costs? This information is for people going from London or Manchester to New York. The prices include the air flight and the hotel.

★ Which is the most expensive time of the year? And which is the cheapest time of the year?
★ If you wanted to stay in New York for 14 nights, when would you go and which hotel would you stay in? Why?

USA from £435 NEW YORK

MANHATTAN

CONSULATE
The Consulate offers 225 spacious and pleasantly furnished guest rooms. It is conveniently located at 224 West 49th Street in the midst of New York's Broadway theatre district and close to many of the city's famous restaurants and stores. Close by is a reasonably priced coffee shop and Wally's restaurant and bar for more formal dining.
ACCOMMODATION: *In rooms with private bath, shower, wc and air conditioning.* MEALS: *Not included.*

WALDORF ASTORIA
Renowned as one of New York's grandest and most distinguished hotels the 1785 room Waldorf Astoria is located on elegant Park Avenue at 50th Street, conveniently close to the Rockefeller Centre, Fifth Avenue shopping and all entertainments. All the amenities of a world class hotel, with restaurants, including the elegant Peacock Alley and less formal Oscar's Coffee House, bars, hairdressing salons and shops.
ACCOMMODATION: *In rooms with private bath, shower, wc and air conditioning.* MEALS: *Not included.*

BARBIZON PLAZA
Enjoying one of New York's most attractive locations on Central Park South, just one block from fashionable Fifth Avenue, the 800 room Barbizon Plaza Hotel is conveniently placed for shopping and sightseeing. For dining, the "Inn the Park" restaurant offers fine cuisine in attractive surroundings, while the Library discothèque provides the ideal after dinner setting.
ACCOMMODATION: *In rooms with private bath, shower, wc and air conditioning.* MEALS: *Not included.*

Average	MONTHLY RAINFALL INS.	MONTHLY HUMIDITY %
Jan	3½	66
Feb	3½	64
Mar	3¾	63
Apr	3¼	62
May	3¼	65
Jun	3¼	67
Jul	4¼	68
Aug	4¼	70
Sep	3½	70
Oct	3½	67
Nov	3	66
Dec	3¼	66

HOLIDAY PRICES Per Person
Departures from London: Every Monday and Saturday Nov 2 1985 to Nov 29 1986
from Manchester: Every Monday and Friday Nov 1 1985 to Nov 28 1986

		Nov 1 to Dec 9	Dec 13 to Dec 23	Dec 27 to Mar 31	Apr 4 to May 31 to Oct 31	Jun 2 to Sep 29	Nov 1 to Nov 29	Supplement for Extra Night	Single Room
Number of Nights		7	7	7	7	7	7	1	1
Hol. No.	In twin room	£	£	£	£	£	£	£	£
S756-01	Consulate	435	540	453	518	540	435	21	21
S756-09	Barbizon Plaza	505	615	527	590	612	510	31	31
S756-04	Waldorf Astoria	620	735	655	717	740	628	49	49

Child Reductions: 2-11 yrs 45%; 12-15 yrs 10%
Air Travel Supplement: Friday & Saturday departures £40.

The Cost includes:
■ Air travel in tourist class from London (or Manchester) to New York and return ■ Hotel accommodation as described ■ Hotel taxes (except $2.00 per room per night occupancy tax at Waldorf Astoria during period

Golden West Tour

★ Which would be the most interesting day for you on this tour? Would you enjoy all the days? Is it a holiday you would like to have? What are the disadvantages of a holiday like this?

(From an American Airplan brochure)

GOLDEN WEST TOUR

Yosemite National Park

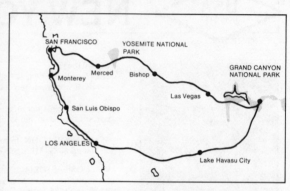

A 14 night tour capturing the Splendour of the Golden West – from the glamour of Los Angeles and Hollywood, and the style and elegance of San Francisco, to the magnificent scenery of the Grand Canyon and Yosemite National Park, and the rugged beauty of the Pacific Coast. Add to this the fun of Disneyland and the excitement of Las Vegas and you have the holiday of a lifetime.

Day 1 – Friday: UK – Los Angeles Your holiday begins as you check in for your Transamerica Airlines flight to Los Angeles. After clearing immigration and customs on arrival, you will be met by the Airplan representative and taken by coach to the hotel Figueroa, your base for the next four nights.

Day 2 – Saturday: In Los Angeles A morning sightseeing tour takes you to Beverly Hills and Hollywood, seeing many of the famous sights and homes of the movie stars. The afternoon and evening are free for you to explore the many attractions of this exciting city.

Day 3 – Sunday: Visit to Disneyland. Your coach will leave today for the Magic Kingdom of Disneyland. You will receive your admission ticket and full day passport to the fabulous adventures and Disneyland is yours to enjoy. Your coach will return you to your hotel in the evening.

Day 4 – Monday: In Los Angeles A free day to enjoy Los Angeles. Your Airplan representative will be on hand to assist you in organising excursions or car hire. This is the ideal day to visit San Diego, perhaps venturing south of the border to the Mexican town of Tijuana (don't forget your passport). In the evening sample the restaurants of L.A.'s Chinatown or Olvira Street – the Mexican heart of Old Los Angeles.

Day 5 – Tuesday: Los Angeles – Lake Havasu An early start today as your tour gets underway heading east through the Mojave Desert and the mountains of Western Arizona, to Lake Havasu City on the Colorado River, the home of old London Bridge. Overnight at the Rodeway Inn.

Day 6 – Wednesday: Lake Havasu – Grand Canyon A morning's drive takes you via Kingman and Williams to the Grand Canyon National Park. The afternoon is free for you to explore the South Rim. During the summer months a free shuttle bus allows you to travel several miles along the rim to view the Canyon from many different points. Overnight at the Motor Lodge Hi-rise.

Day 7 – Thursday: At Grand Canyon A full day to enjoy the splendour of the Grand Canyon; perhaps you will take a helicopter ride to view nature's wonder from above, or take a hike to the Colorado River hundreds of feet below the Rim (please seek the advice of the Rangers before venturing down).

Day 8 – Friday: Grand Canyon – Las Vegas Another day of magnificent scenery as your tour heads towards the entertainment centre of the West – Las Vegas. Stopping en route to view the mighty Hoover Dam, you should arrive at the Riviera Hotel on the famous 'Strip' in time to relax before exploring the lights, shows and casinos of Las Vegas.

Day 9 – Saturday: Las Vegas – Bishop Leaving Las Vegas this morning, the tour continues west through Nevada, close to Death Valley, before reaching Bishop in the early evening. Overnight at the Travelodge, Bishop.

Day 10 – Sunday: Bishop – Yosemite – Merced Today's journey is through the lakeside town of Lee Vining, then over Tioga Pass (weather permitting) into the High Sierra Mountains and Yosemite National Park, probably the most spectacular area of concentrated beauty in North America. Your hotel for tonight will be the Travelodge at Merced.

Day 11 – Monday: Merced – San Francisco Having already viewed much of the Park the previous day, today's tour is devoted to

Yosemite Valley with its mighty peaks, plunging waterfalls and Giant Sequoia Trees. After the tour the coach takes you through the California fruit growing region to San Francisco. Your hotel for the next three nights is the Californian.

Day 12 – Tuesday: In San Francisco A morning sightseeing tour takes in many of San Francisco's famous landmarks, Chinatown, Union Square, Fisherman's Wharf, Golden Gate Bridge and much more. The afternoon is free for you to explore at leisure.

Day 13 – Wednesday: In San Francisco From your hotel ideally situated in the downtown area, you are free to enjoy this beautiful city. Your Airplan representative will be on hand to assist you in planning your day.

Day 14 – Thursday: San Francisco – San Luis Obispo Travelling south today your tour takes the coastal road of the Monterey Peninsula and the famous 17 Mile Drive with its spectacular views of the rugged Pacific coast. Through the artist's haven of Carmel the tour continues to San Luis Obispo right on the coast, and your hotel, the Howard Johnson Lodge.

Day 15 – Friday: San Luis Obispo – Los Angeles The final leg of the tour takes you inland through Southern California arriving at Los Angeles Airport in time to check in for your overnight flight to the U.K. Dinner will be served on board, then you can relax, enjoy the movie before breakfast and arrival in U.K.

Day 16 – Saturday: Tour ends Your tour ends today on arrival at your U.K. airport.

Las Vegas

Grand Canyon

Last thoughts

For millions of years people lived in small groups and travelled about hunting for animals and looking for plants, nuts and fruit. And today millions of people travel many millions of kilometres for work, pleasure, to avoid war, to join their families or just to explore.

I hope that you have found information in this book which will help you to travel successfully. You may have got some ideas for your holidays, you may have found out how to get cheap fares for your journey, how to protect yourself from thieves, from the heat of the desert or from getting lost in London! And I hope you will have improved your English! English is a very useful possession when you travel.

If you would like to learn more information about other subjects and improve your English then you may be interested to know that there are four other books in this series – all of them are useful to the successful traveller!

Answers

Page 47

C – 760330
D – 758303
E – 742313

Page 49

Some of these questions are easy and some are difficult. The number at the end of each answer is for full marks! You can give yourself half marks if you get the answer half right! Add up all your points. If you have more than 50 you are a brilliant map reader, if you have between 40 and 49 you are quite good, if you have between 25 and 39 you need practice, if you have less than 24 you will need a lot of help from local people!

1 459265 (2 points)
2 You go to the main road and turn right. You go along the road for about two kilometres until you come to the village of Pooley Bridge. You go through the village and over the bridge.

You go along the road for a few hundred metres and you will find the pier on your left. (4 points)

3 Three (1 point)

4 Two (1 point)

5 Yes (1 point)

6 Yes (1 point)

7 A hill with trees on it (2 points)

8 Three (2 points)

9 In Dacre there is a church with a tower, in Barton a church with a tower as well and in Pooley Bridge a church with a spire. (3 points)

10 No (1 point)

11 There is a school in Dacre. (1 point)

12 There is a telephone at Souland Gate. Go right down the road. After a kilometre it turns sharp left but you must go straight on. You will find the telephone in the first lane on your left. (2 points)

13 I think it is the little road which goes out of Pooley Bridge and up past the Howe Hill caravan site to Roehead. (4 points)

14 No (1 point)

15 Go onto the road and turn right. After about two kilometres turn left into Pooley Bridge village, past the church, over the bridge, round the hill then turn right. At the top of the hill there is a T junction. You must turn left there and you will come to Dacre after about two kilometres. (4 points)

16 No, there is a hill on the other side of the lake. Dacre is on the other side of the hill and is not as high as the hill. (4 points)

17 Yes (1 point)

18 You can walk to Barton. (1 point)

19 Yes (1 point)

20 There are a lot of old places, for example, there is a castle at Dacre. There is a Roman road to the east of Pooley Bridge and this passes stone sites. (4 points for this answer or for other choices)

21 Most of the woods aren't mixed but there are some south of Dacre (West Park). (2 points)

22 About 150 metres. (3 points)

23 Dacre is lower than the stone circle. (3 points)

24 The church has a spire and it is on the right. We pass a few houses and then come to a crossroads. We go straight across and the road begins to go up the hill. There is a camp and caravan site on our left, and a little later some quarries. We continue past a very small wood on our right. At last we come to the moor where the grass is wet. We are on a path now and it climbs steeply up the hill until we come to the Roman road. We turn right for a few hundred metres, we cross a small stream and then arrive at the stone circle. (5 points)

25 About four kilometres. (2 points)

Acknowledgements

The author and publishers are grateful to the following individuals, companies and institutions who have given permission for the use of copyright material identified in the text. It has not been possible to identify the sources of all the material used and in such cases the publishers would welcome information from copyright owners.

John Reader for the photograph on p. 1; American Express Europe Ltd for the material on pp. 8–9; the staff of Thomas Cook Ltd, Yeovil, for their help in checking facts and prices on pp. 18–19; Britannia Airways Ltd for the photograph on p. 29; Polysales Gifts for the text and illustration at the bottom of p. 36; Ordnance Survey for the map on p. 48; West Yorkshire Metropolitan County Council from whose publication 'Stop yourself dying on the moors' the information on p. 50 has been adapted; Barry Jones for the photographs of Annie and Reg Stainer on p. 64; Britain on View Photo Library (British Tourist Authority) for the photographs on pp. 65 (top), 66 (middle), 67 (bottom left), 74; Barnaby's Picture Library for the photographs on pp. 65 (middle), 66 (top left, bottom); Eurocruisers for the photograph and boat plan on p. 68; Butlins for the material on p. 69; PGL Young Adventure Ltd and Millfield School Enterprises Ltd for the photographs and text on pp. 71–73; Wales Tourist Board for the photograph and information on p. 75; Youth Hostels Association (England and Wales) for the photograph on p. 76 (middle); Red Lion Hotel, Clovelly for the photograph on p. 77; American Airplan for the brochure information on pp. 79–80 and pp. 82–83; Speedbird Holidays for the brochure information on p. 81. Other photographs are by the author.